LIFE NOW & BEYOND

Prepare today. Be ready for tomorrow.

A complete teaching companion for the Life Now & Beyond course.

TEACHER'S GUIDE

Helping Adults Understand,
Prepare, and Find Peace of Mind

COMPANION TO

When a Loved One Dies

and

Not My Favorite Subject Either, But...

by Alice Truman

Companion app · lifenowandbeyond.com

First Edition, 2026

ISBN: 978-1-968871-96-3

Top Artists 4 U LLC
15021 Ventura Blvd. #783
Sherman Oaks, CA 91403
TopArtists4U@gmail.com

Important Legal Disclaimer

and Limitation of Liability

Please read this disclaimer carefully before using this guide.

Educational Purpose Only

This guide is designed to provide general information and a structured framework for teaching a community course on grief, loss, and end-of-life preparation. It is sold and distributed with the understanding that neither the author nor the publisher is engaged in rendering legal, financial, medical, tax, mental health, counseling, or other professional services through this guide or the course it supports.

Not Professional Advice

The information contained in this guide and the books it accompanies is for educational and informational purposes only. It is not intended to be, and should not be construed as, professional advice or recommendations specific to any individual's circumstances. Laws, regulations, medical practices, and best practices vary significantly by state, country, and jurisdiction, and change frequently. Before making any decisions or taking any actions based on information in this guide, the course, or the companion books, participants should consult qualified licensed professionals, including but not limited to licensed attorneys, certified financial planners, licensed physicians, certified public accountants, and licensed mental health professionals.

Teacher Status

Any person teaching this course using this guide does so as a facilitator of educational content, not as a licensed professional. Regardless of any teacher's individual professional background or credentials, the teacher is not acting in a professional capacity when teaching this course. Use of this guide does not create any attorney-client relationship, doctor-patient relationship, financial advisory relationship, or therapeutic relationship between any teacher and any participant. Teachers using this guide assume responsibility for their own conduct of the course and agree to follow the sensitivity guidance and professional referral guidance contained in this guide.

Educational and Supportive, Not Therapeutic

This course is educational and supportive in nature. It is not group therapy, grief counseling, or mental health treatment. Participants experiencing acute grief, mental health concerns, suicidal ideation, substance use issues, family crisis, or any other situation requiring professional support should seek qualified help from licensed professionals. Teachers are instructed to refer participants to appropriate professionals and emergency resources, including the 988 Suicide and Crisis Lifeline, when warning signs are present.

Confidentiality Limitations

While the course establishes confidentiality as a ground rule for participants, no community course can guarantee what other participants will or will not share outside the room. Participants share personal information at their own discretion and risk.

Reproducible Handouts

Pages of this guide that are explicitly marked as reproducible handouts may be photocopied by purchasers of this guide for use with participants in their own courses. No other portion of this guide may be reproduced or distributed without written permission. The handouts may not be sold, posted publicly, or distributed outside of a course context.

Relationship to Books and App

This guide is a companion resource to the books *When a Loved One Dies* and *Not My Favorite Subject Either, But...*, both by Alice Truman, and to the LifeNowAndBeyond.com companion app. This guide is not a substitute for the books or the app. Use of the LifeNowAndBeyond.com app is governed by separate terms of use found on that website.

Limitation of Liability

To the fullest extent permitted by law, the author and publisher specifically disclaim any liability, loss, or risk, personal or otherwise, which is incurred as a consequence, directly or indirectly, of the use or application of any of the contents of this guide. Neither the author nor the publisher shall be liable for any damages arising from the use of, reliance on, or inability to use information contained in this guide or any course taught using this guide.

Your Responsibility

You are responsible for seeking appropriate professional guidance for your specific circumstances and for the circumstances of any participants in your course. By using this guide, you acknowledge that you do so at your own risk and agree to take responsibility for your own decisions and conduct.

This Teacher's Guide belongs to:

____

(Your Name)

Teach. Guide. Support. Make a difference.

Table of Contents

Sections, modules, and reproducible handouts are listed below. Page numbers refer to this teacher's guide; chapter assignments for the two companion books appear within each module.

BEFORE YOU TEACH

THE SIX MODULES

AFTER THE COURSE

PART ONE

BEFORE YOU TEACH

Everything you need to know before you teach.

Welcome, Teacher

Thank you for stepping into one of the most meaningful roles a person can take on in a community: helping people face death honestly, with both their hearts and their hands. The course you are about to lead is built around two simple truths.

The first truth is that everyone we love will die, and we will too. The second truth is that almost no one is prepared for either, and that lack of preparation makes an already painful experience harder than it needs to be.

This course exists to bridge that gap. Over six weeks, you will guide a small group of people through a journey that touches the practical, the emotional, and the relational dimensions of death and grief. Some of your participants may be facing the recent loss of someone they love. Others may be preparing for their own eventual death and trying to spare their families the chaos that unprepared deaths leave behind. Many will be doing both at once. All of them will leave this course with more clarity, more peace, and more practical tools than they had when they walked in.

You do not need to be a counselor, a clergy member, a lawyer, or a funeral professional to teach this course. You need to be a person willing to sit with hard topics, hold space for grief, and walk a small group of people through material that has been organized for you week by week. Everything you need is in this guide.

A FEW THINGS TO KNOW BEFORE YOU BEGIN

This course is **secular and broadly applicable**. It works in churches, community centers, hospices, libraries, senior centers, funeral homes, workplaces, and private homes. The content does not assume any particular faith tradition, though it does not avoid spiritual topics when they arise naturally in discussion. You can adapt the tone for your setting.

This course draws from **two books by Alice Truman**: *When a Loved One Dies* (focused on what to do after a death) and *Not My Favorite Subject Either, But...* (focused on planning before death). Most participants will own at least one of the books. Some will own both. Each module includes specific reading assignments from both books, and the course works whether participants have one or both.

This course also has a **digital companion**: the LifeNowAndBeyond.com app. The app provides interactive tools, planning templates, and resources that complement the printed material. References to the app appear throughout this guide where they fit naturally.

Above all, this course is meant to be practical. By week six, your participants will have begun real planning, real conversations, and real movement through their own grief. That is the whole point. You are not teaching theory. You are helping people do something that genuinely matters.

> "*Welcome. Take a breath. Let us begin.*"

About This Course

What Participants Will Learn

Over six weekly sessions, participants will:

- Understand why our culture avoids talking about death and how to begin those conversations with the people who matter most
- Learn the practical steps that need to happen in the first hours, days, and weeks after a loved one dies
- Begin organizing the legal, financial, medical, and digital information their own families will need someday
- Recognize the emotional and relational dynamics that grief brings out in families and develop strategies for navigating them
- Build a personal plan for both end-of-life preparation and grief support that they can continue refining long after the course ends

Who This Course Is For

This course is designed for the everyday adult who wants to face death and grief with more readiness than our culture typically provides. That includes:

- People who are currently grieving and want practical guidance alongside emotional support
- People who are caring for an aging or seriously ill loved one and want to be prepared for what is coming
- People who want to spare their own families the chaos and conflict that unprepared deaths create
- People who simply recognize that they do not know what they do not know, and want to fix that before they need to

The course is appropriate for adults of any age. Younger adults often appreciate the planning content because they have aging parents. Older adults often appreciate the planning content because they want to leave their affairs in order. Everyone benefits from the grief content, because grief comes for everyone eventually.

Who This Course Is Not For

This course is not therapy. It is not a substitute for grief counseling, mental health treatment, legal advice, or financial planning. Participants who are in acute grief, severe depression, or any kind of mental health crisis need professional support that this course cannot provide. As the teacher, you will learn to recognize these situations and refer participants to qualified professionals. There is detailed guidance on this in a later section.

How This Course Was Built from the Books

Alice Truman's two books cover the full arc of how a family handles death. Together they answer two questions every adult eventually faces:

> *What do I do when someone I love dies?*
> *How do I prepare so my family is not lost when I die?*

This course brings both questions together in a six-week journey. Each module draws content from one or both books, organized into a sequence that works whether a participant is grieving now, planning for the future, or both.

How the Modules Map to the Books

A general guide to the source material for each module is below. Specific chapter assignments are listed within each module of this guide.

- **Module 1** (The Conversation We Avoid) draws from the introductions of both books and the early chapters of *Not My Favorite Subject Either, But...*
- **Module 2** (Getting Your Affairs in Order) draws primarily from *Not My Favorite Subject Either, But...*, Chapters 3 through 6
- **Module 3** (The Immediate Aftermath) draws primarily from *When a Loved One Dies*, Chapters 1 through 3
- **Module 4** (Documents, Legal Matters, and Digital Life) draws from *When a Loved One Dies*, Chapters 4 through 6, and *Not My Favorite Subject Either, But...*, Chapters 7 through 9
- **Module 5** (Grief, Family, and Self-Care) draws from *When a Loved One Dies*, Chapters 7 through 11, and *Not My Favorite Subject Either, But...*, Chapters 10 and 11
- **Module 6** (Moving Forward and Leaving a Legacy) draws from *When a Loved One Dies*, Chapters 12 and 13, and *Not My Favorite Subject Either, But...*, Chapter 12

What If a Participant Only Has One Book?

The course is designed so that every participant gains real value regardless of which book or books they own.

- A participant with only *When a Loved One Dies* will find Modules 3 through 6 most directly aligned with their reading and will treat the planning content in Modules 1 and 2 as preview material that may motivate them to acquire the second book later.

- A participant with only *Not My Favorite Subject Either, But...* will find Modules 1, 2, and parts of 4 through 6 most directly aligned with their reading and will treat the aftermath content in Module 3 as preview material that may motivate them to acquire the second book later.
- A participant with both books will move smoothly through all six modules with full reading support.

Each module in this guide tells you, the teacher, exactly which chapters to assign for each scenario. You do not need to figure this out on your own.

How to Use This Guide

Read This Guide All the Way Through Before You Teach

Before your first session, read this entire guide once. You do not need to memorize anything, but you should know the shape of all six modules so you can see how the course builds. This is especially important for the early modules, where you will sometimes need to acknowledge content that is coming later.

How Each Module Is Structured

Every module in this guide follows the same predictable pattern, so once you teach Module 1, you will know exactly what to expect for the rest of the course. Each module contains:

- **Module Overview** — a one-page summary of what the session covers and what participants will leave with
- **Learning Objectives** — what participants should know or be able to do by the end of the session
- **Materials Needed** — a checklist of what to bring and prepare
- **Lesson Plan with Timing** — a recommended schedule for the session
- **Teacher's Script and Talking Points** — language you can read aloud or paraphrase, with the teaching content broken into manageable pieces
- **Discussion Questions** — more questions than you will need, so you can choose what fits your group
- **In-Class Activity** — a structured exercise that gets participants doing something, not just listening
- **Reading Assignments for Next Week** — clear chapter assignments from both books
- **App Integration** — specific ways to use the LifeNowAndBeyond.com app to extend the lesson
- **Sensitivity Notes** — what to watch for emotionally during this particular session
- **Reproducible Handouts** — one or more pages you can photocopy for participants

How to Adapt the Material to Your Group

No two groups are the same. A group of widows in their seventies will not respond to the material the same way as a group of working professionals in their forties. As the teacher, you have permission to adapt.

You can shorten the teaching segments and lengthen the discussion if your group is talkative and processes by speaking. You can lengthen the teaching segments and shorten the discussion if your group is quieter and prefers to absorb. You can substitute a personal story of your own for one of the suggested examples if it fits the moment. You can skip an activity if the conversation has already accomplished what the activity was meant to accomplish.

WHAT YOU SHOULD NOT DO

Skip the reading assignments, skip the sensitivity notes, or skip the professional referral guidance. Those are the spine of the course.

The Books and the App

When a Loved One Dies

This is the aftermath book. It is built for people who are dealing with a death right now or who want to be prepared for one that is coming. The book covers the first 24 hours, the next 72 hours, the planning of services, the documents and legal matters that follow, the digital life of the deceased, and the grief journey through and beyond the funeral. It includes quick-reference checklists and templates throughout.

Chapter assignments from this book appear in Modules 3, 4, 5, and 6 of this course.

Not My Favorite Subject Either, But...

This is the preparation book. It is built for people who want to get their own affairs in order so their loved ones are not left in chaos. It is part guide and part workbook, with reflection prompts, worksheets, and checklists that participants can complete as they go. The book covers legal must-haves, money matters, health and end-of-life choices, funeral and memorial planning, digital legacy, personal legacy projects, organizing a final binder, talking with loved ones, emotional and spiritual closure, and living well until the end.

Chapter assignments from this book appear in Modules 1, 2, 4, 5, and 6 of this course.

The Life Now and Beyond App

The companion app at *lifenowandbeyond.com* is the digital extension of both books. From the Home Dashboard, two main paths organize the app: **Before Someone Passes Away** and **After Someone Has Passed Away**. From the bottom navigation, participants can reach the Life Binder, the Planning Journal, the Resource hub, and Settings.

Features Participants Will Use Most Often During This Course

The Life Binder is the heart of the app. It is organized into seven categories: Personal Information, Medical Information, Insurance Policies, Financial Information, Legal Documents, Final Wishes, and Digital Legacy. Each category lets the user record entries that build a complete picture of what their family will eventually need.

Trusted Access lets the user designate trusted people who can reach the Life Binder in an emergency. The user assigns each contact a permission level: Medical Information Only, Legal Documents Only, Financial Overview Only, or Full Emergency Access. This is the feature that turns the app from a private organizer into a real family protection system.

The Before Journey is an eight-chapter guided walk through the territory of personal preparation. Each chapter has a brief reflection, journal prompts, and a small-steps checklist. Participants use this between sessions to deepen the work the course covers in person.

The Life Planning Checklist is an interactive checklist covering Important Contacts, Important Documents, Medical Information, Insurance Information, and Financial Accounts, with the ability to add custom items.

Conversation Starters are prompts designed to help families have the difficult but necessary conversations the course is helping participants prepare for. Participants will draw on these in Module 5.

The Planning Journal is a private reflective space for notes, family observations, planning thoughts, and legacy reflections.

The Resource hub contains articles (which open on the Life Now & Beyond website), the Books page, the Emergency Resources page (988, Crisis Text Line, NAMI, GriefShare), and a set of Guided Support Tools (Grounding 5-4-3-2-1, I'm Overwhelmed, Guided Calming Message, and Comfort Message Cards).

The After-Loss Guidance & Support workspace is a structured 22-step interactive tool for navigating the time after a loss. It includes Immediate Steps, a Who to Notify checklist, Documents to Gather, Funeral Planning, Grief Journal prompts, an Emotional Support entry, and a Remembrance entry. This workspace is one of the app's deepest features.

Remembrance is the part of the app where users and families can create memorial pages with photos, stories, tributes, and legacy reflections.

Free Tier and Premium

The app is offered with a free tier and a premium subscription. The free tier is meaningful and substantial – it includes the full Home Dashboard, Trusted Access for up to 3 contacts, three Life Binder sections (Personal Information, Medical Information, and Final Wishes), the full Before Journey, the full Life Planning Checklist, full access to articles and emergency resources, three of the four Guided Support Tools, a starter set of Conversation Starters, and the basic Planning Journal. Participants can do real, meaningful work in the free tier through the early modules of this course.

Premium ($5.99 per month or $49 per year) adds the four remaining Life Binder sections (Insurance Policies, Financial Information, Legal Documents, and Digital Legacy), document uploads with secure storage, unlimited Trusted Access contacts, the full After-Loss Guidance & Support 22-step workspace, the full Conversation Starters library, Remembrance Pages creation, expanded journal features, the full caregiver toolkit, and premium grief support resources. Premium is what completes the protection promise: the user's trusted contacts can only see Life Binder sections the user has been able to populate, and four of the seven sections require premium to fill.

A NOTE FOR TEACHERS

Throughout this guide, App Integration prompts suggest specific ways to use the app between sessions. You do not need to require the app or premium for participants to benefit from this course. But you should mention the app consistently as a resource, and you should be honest about what each tier provides so participants can make informed choices about whether and when to upgrade.

How the App Pacing Works

This course is designed to work in synchronization with the Life Now & Beyond app. Participants who download the app at the start of the course can use the free tier to complete most of the early work; as the course moves into the deeper preparation territory in the back half, premium features become more directly useful. The pacing is intentional and graceful – it lets participants experience the app at every stage and make their own decision about when, or whether, to upgrade.

Modules 1 Through 3: The Free Tier Carries Participants

The first half of the course is fully achievable on the free tier of the app. Participants set up their accounts in Module 1, begin populating the three free Life Binder sections (Personal Information, Medical Information, and Final Wishes) in Module 2, and read the free articles on the first 24 hours and the next 72 hours in Module 3. They can begin the Before Journey, use the Life Planning Checklist, configure up to three Trusted Access contacts, and explore most of the Guided Support Tools – all without paying anything.

In Module 2, participants will discover that three of the four pillars of preparation in the Life Binder are partially or fully premium-gated: Legal Documents, Financial Information, and Insurance Policies. This is intentional. The course teaches them what they need; the app shows them where the boundary is. The conversation about whether to upgrade should not be forced in Module 2 – just acknowledge the boundary honestly when it comes up.

Module 4: The Natural Conversion Moment

Module 4 is where premium features start to matter directly. The module covers Documents, Legal Matters, and Digital Life. The Digital Legacy section of the Life Binder is premium-only. The Trusted Access feature, which participants have already configured with up to three contacts, becomes a much deeper conversation in this module: trusted contacts can only see the Life Binder sections the user has been able to populate, which on the free tier is three of seven. Premium completes the protection.

The Module 4 teacher's script includes language for handling this moment gracefully. The framing is not "you must upgrade." It is "this is the natural week where premium features become valuable, and the choice is yours."

Modules 5 and 6: Premium Adds Depth, Free Still Works

Module 5 uses Conversation Starters, where the free starter set is enough for the activity but premium adds substantial depth (specialized prompts for blended families, estranged relationships, business succession, and so on). Module 6 introduces Remembrance Pages, which require premium to create but can be viewed on free.

A participant who never upgrades can still complete every module's in-class activity. A participant who upgrades after Module 4 will find the second half of the course significantly richer.

What This Means for You as the Teacher

You do not need to sell the app or premium. The app does its own work. Your job is to mention the app consistently as a resource, to be honest about which tier supports which work, and to trust that participants who find the app useful will upgrade when it makes sense for them.

The App Integration sections in each module of this guide are written with this in mind. They tell participants what to do in the app between sessions, they note when an activity may bump into a premium feature, and they offer language for participants who want to know more about what premium adds.

Sensitivity Guidance

for Teaching This Material

This course touches some of the most painful experiences a human being can have. As the teacher, you are not expected to fix anyone or carry anyone, but you are expected to create a room where people can be honest about what they are going through. This section gives you the tools to do that.

What to Expect Emotionally in Your Sessions

You should plan for the following to happen at some point during your six weeks together. None of these are problems. They are signs the course is working.

- **Someone will cry.** Possibly several people, possibly more than once. Tears are not a crisis. They are appropriate to the material.
- **Someone will share a story that moves the entire room.** Let it land. Do not rush past it.
- **Someone will become angry**, often at a family member who has not done their share, or at a deceased person who left a mess behind. Anger in grief is normal and does not need to be argued with.
- **Someone will laugh**, sometimes about something dark. Grief humor is real and healthy. Let it happen.
- **Someone will go quiet** for a whole session. Do not press them. They are still receiving.
- **Someone will share more than the group can hold.** You will need to gently redirect.

Ground Rules to Establish in Module 1

In your first session, you will establish four ground rules with your participants. These hold up the room for the rest of the course.

1. **What is shared here stays here.** Confidentiality is non-negotiable. Names, situations, and stories shared in the room belong only to the people in the room.
2. **You are never required to share.** Anyone can pass on any question or activity at any time without explanation.
3. **We are not here to fix each other.** Advice-giving and problem-solving are not the goals. Listening and witnessing are.
4. **We use respectful language.** We avoid judging anyone for how they grieve, what they believe, what their family is like, or what they have or have not done to prepare.

Handling Emotional Moments

When someone gets emotional during the session, your job is straightforward. Pause. Acknowledge. Continue when ready. You do not need to make a speech. You do not need to interpret what is happening. A simple, "Take your time. We are with you," is often all that is required.

If someone needs to step out, let them. If they do not return for several minutes, briefly check on them at a natural break, but do not force them back into the room.

If the whole group becomes heavy, it is okay to say so. A line like, "This is a lot. Let us take a breath together," can reset the room. A literal pause of even thirty seconds is more useful than pushing through.

What You Are Not

You are not a therapist. You are not a counselor. You are not a lawyer, a financial advisor, or a funeral director. When participants present situations that go beyond what this course can address, your job is to refer them, not to advise them. The next section tells you how.

When to Refer a Participant

for Professional Support

A small number of participants in any grief or end-of-life course will be in situations that need professional help beyond what a community course can offer. Your job is not to diagnose anyone. Your job is to recognize warning signs and gently encourage participants to seek qualified support.

Mental Health Concerns

If a participant shows any of the following, encourage them to speak with a mental health professional:

- Persistent inability to function in daily life weeks or months after a loss
- Expressions of wanting to die, not wanting to live, or wishing they had died with the person they lost
- Severe sleep disruption, weight changes, or substance use that has emerged or worsened since the loss
- Complete social withdrawal that does not improve over time
- Disturbing or intrusive thoughts that the participant describes as scary or overwhelming

IF A PARTICIPANT EXPRESSES THOUGHTS OF SELF-HARM

Take it seriously. Speak with the person privately after the session.
Provide the **988 Suicide and Crisis Lifeline** (call or text 988).
Encourage them to contact their primary care doctor, a mental health professional, or a crisis line that day.
If you believe they are in immediate danger, stay with them and help them connect to emergency support.
Do not leave them alone.
You are not their counselor. You are a person who noticed and cared enough to act.

Legal and Financial Concerns

Many participants will have specific legal or financial questions about wills, trusts, probate, taxes, real estate, or insurance. You are not qualified to answer these, and even if you happen to be qualified in your day job, this is not the setting to do so. Refer participants to:

- A licensed attorney for any estate, probate, or family-law question
- A certified financial planner or accountant for any financial or tax question

- A licensed insurance professional for insurance questions

> *That is a great question for an attorney who knows your state. The course can point you toward what to ask. It cannot give you the answer.*

Medical and End-of-Life Care

When a participant is dealing with serious illness, hospice decisions, or healthcare directives in real time, those questions belong with their healthcare team, a hospice social worker, or a healthcare proxy. The course can support them emotionally and with general information. It cannot substitute for clinical guidance.

Family Conflict That Has Become Toxic

Some participants will be in family situations involving estrangement, abuse, exploitation, or legal disputes around an estate. These are real and painful, but they go beyond what a six-week course can resolve.

Encourage these participants to seek a family mediator, a therapist who works with families, or an attorney depending on the nature of the conflict.

Setting Up Your Course

Group Size

The ideal group size is six to twelve participants. Smaller groups can feel exposed when emotions are high. Larger groups limit how much each person can share. If you have more than twelve interested participants, consider running two groups in sequence rather than combining them into one.

Space

You need a private room where conversations cannot be overheard. Comfortable chairs in a circle or around a table work better than rows facing the front. Tissues should be visible and accessible. Water should be available.

Materials Each Participant Needs

- At least one of the two books (*When a Loved One Dies* and/or *Not My Favorite Subject Either, But...*)
- A notebook or journal for personal reflection between sessions
- A pen
- Optional: access to the LifeNowAndBeyond.com app

Materials You Need as the Teacher

- This Teacher's Guide
- Copies of all reproducible handouts for each session
- A timer or clock visible to you
- Tissues
- A name tag or table tent for each participant if your group does not already know each other
- A sign-in sheet so you can follow up with anyone who misses a session

Before Your First Session (Suggested)

1. Read this entire guide.
2. Read both books, even if you have already read them once. Pay particular attention to the chapters assigned in each module.
3. Download the Life Now & Beyond app yourself, set up an account, and explore it. You should be familiar enough with the app to walk participants through onboarding in Module 1.
4. Confirm the meeting space has reliable Wi-Fi for app downloads in Module 1.
5. Photocopy the Module 1 handouts.
6. Identify a quiet, private space and confirm it is reserved for all six weeks.
7. Send participants a welcome message confirming the start date, location, time, and what to bring — including their smartphone for Module 1's app onboarding.

On Timing and Flexibility

Each module in this guide is designed for a recommended session length of **60 minutes**. In practice, many sessions will run a little long, especially the early ones, because grief and end-of-life topics open up real conversations and real conversations take time.

> *This is not a problem. It is the work.*

At the same time, predictability matters. Participants need to be able to plan their evenings. They need to know that when you say a session is 60 minutes, you mean it. Here is how to hold both truths at once.

Book the Room for 90 Minutes

Even though the course is designed for 60-minute sessions, reserve your meeting space for 90 minutes every week. This gives you a buffer for the sessions that need it, without forcing you to cut conversations short or kick participants out when the door is being unlocked for the next group.

Aim to End at 60 Minutes

Plan to wrap by the 60-minute mark whenever possible. Most weeks, you will be able to. The discipline of ending on time teaches participants that this is a structured experience they can rely on, and it respects the lives they are returning to after class.

Allow Sessions to Run to 90 Minutes Only When the Moment Calls for It

Occasionally, a session will need 75 or 90 minutes. Someone shares something that the group needs to honor. A discussion catches fire and is producing real insight. A participant arrives in fresh grief and the room needs to receive them. In moments like these, it is appropriate to extend. Tell the group, "We are going to take a few extra minutes tonight. If you need to leave at the hour, please do, and we will see you next week."

Never go past 90 minutes. If a topic clearly needs more time than that, save it for next week rather than running long tonight.

Advertise the Course Honestly

When you promote the course, describe it as "weekly 60 to 90 minute sessions." This sets expectations honestly and matches the rhythm of most evening community classes. You will lose fewer participants to scheduling concerns when they know what they are committing to.

Where Each Module Has Natural Flex Points

In every module, the lesson plan has one or two segments where running long is most natural and most useful. These are usually the discussion segment and, in Module 1, the introductions. Within the timing table for each module, the recommended session length is given as a range, and you will see notes throughout the script about where it is safe to let things breathe.

Six-Module Overview

at a Glance

A summary of what each module covers, what participants take home, and which book chapters anchor the session.

Module 1 — The Conversation We Avoid

Why our culture avoids talking about death, what it costs us, and how this course will help. Establishes ground rules, builds the group, and motivates the work ahead.

Reading: Reading from *Not My Favorite Subject Either, But...*, Chapters 1 and 2.

Module 2 — Getting Your Affairs in Order

Wills, trusts, financial documents, healthcare directives, funeral planning. The practical preparation that turns chaos into clarity for the people we love.

Reading: Reading from *Not My Favorite Subject Either, But...*, Chapters 3 through 6.

Module 3 — The Immediate Aftermath

What happens in the first 24 hours, the next 72 hours, and the planning of services. Step-by-step practical guidance for one of the most disorienting moments in a person's life.

Reading: Reading from *When a Loved One Dies*, Chapters 1 through 3.

Module 4 — Documents, Legal Matters, and Digital Life

The paperwork that follows a death and the digital legacy that needs handling. Bank accounts, insurance, probate basics, social media, passwords, and online accounts.

Reading: Reading from *When a Loved One Dies*, Chapters 4 through 6, and *Not My Favorite Subject Either, But...*, Chapters 7 through 9.

Module 5 — Grief, Family, and Self-Care

The emotional and relational journey through loss. How grief shows up, how family dynamics shift, how to care for yourself, and how to support others.

Reading: Reading from *When a Loved One Dies*, Chapters 7 through 11, and *Not My Favorite Subject Either, But...*, Chapters 10 and 11.

Module 6 — Moving Forward and Leaving a Legacy

Life after the funeral. Anniversaries, holidays, secondary losses, finding meaning, and the legacy each of us is leaving even now.

Reading: Reading from *When a Loved One Dies*, Chapters 12 and 13, and *Not My Favorite Subject Either, But...*, Chapter 12.

PART TWO

THE SIX MODULES

Your week-by-week teaching companion.

WEEK ONE

MODULE

01

The Conversation We Avoid

Why this conversation matters — and why we have not been having it.

Module Overview

Module 1 sets the foundation for the entire six-week course. Your job in this session is not to teach a lot of content. Your job is to build the group, establish trust, normalize the discomfort that everyone is feeling about discussing death, and motivate the practical work that the next five weeks will demand.

By the end of this session, every participant should know why they are here, what to expect from the course, who else is in the room, and that talking about death is not the morbid undertaking they may have feared.

Many will leave the first session feeling lighter than they expected. That is the goal.

Learning Objectives

By the end of Module 1, participants will be able to:

- Articulate at least two reasons our culture avoids conversations about death
- Identify the personal cost of avoiding those conversations in their own family
- Describe what the next five weeks of the course will cover
- Name at least one specific reason they chose to be in this course
- Begin to see the people around them in the room as fellow travelers, not strangers

Materials Needed

- Teacher's Guide (this document)
- Sign-in sheet
- Name tags or table tents (if participants do not know each other)
- Tissues, visible and accessible
- Water and cups
- A timer or clock
- Reproducible Handout 1A: Welcome and Course Overview (one per participant)
- Reproducible Handout 1B: Why I Am Here (one per participant)
- Reproducible Handout 1C: Reading and Reflection for Week 2 (one per participant)
- A whiteboard, flipchart, or large pad for capturing group input (optional but useful)

CONFIRM BEFORE THE SESSION

Every participant should plan to bring their smartphone to Module 1, and the meeting space should have reliable Wi-Fi for app downloads. Mention this in your reminder email a few days before.

Lesson Plan with Timing

Recommended session length: 60 minutes. Plan for 60 to 90 minutes to allow for natural discussion. **Module 1 is the most likely module to run long because of introductions; reserve the room for the full 90 minutes.**

TIME	SEGMENT	PURPOSE
0:00 – 0:05	**Welcome and Settling**	Greet participants, distribute handouts, set the tone, briefly introduce yourself.
0:05 – 0:15	**Ground Rules and Introductions**	Establish the four ground rules. Each participant says their name and one sentence about why they are here.
0:15 – 0:23	**App Onboarding (Together)**	Walk the group through downloading the Life Now & Beyond app, creating a free account, and a quick orientation tour. Participants leave with the app installed and ready.
0:23 – 0:38	**Teaching Segment: The Conversation We Avoid**	The main teaching content of the module.
0:38 – 0:50	**Discussion**	Open conversation using the discussion questions. Choose two or three; do not try to use all of them. *Flex point — extend by 5 to 10 minutes if the group is engaged.*
0:50 – 0:55	**In-Class Activity: Why I Am Here**	Participants complete Handout 1B. Optional brief sharing.
0:55 – 1:00	**Closing and Preview of Module 2**	Distribute reading assignments. Preview what is coming. Close warmly.

Teacher's Script and Talking Points

What follows is the core content for the session, broken into sections that align with the lesson plan above. The italicized passages are scripted language you can read aloud verbatim or paraphrase in your own voice. The non-italicized text is teaching content with talking points and notes for you.

Welcome and Settling (5 minutes)

As participants arrive, greet them warmly, hand them a name tag if needed, and offer them water. When everyone is seated, take a breath and begin.

> *Welcome, everyone. Thank you for being here. The fact that you walked through that door tonight, knowing what this course is about, tells me something true about you. You are willing to face something most people spend their lives avoiding. That takes courage. Before we go any further, I want to say this clearly: you are in the right room. Whatever brought you here, whatever you are carrying, this is a space where it belongs.*

Briefly introduce yourself. Name, why you are teaching this course, and one sentence about what drew you to the material. Keep it short — under 90 seconds. *The session is not about you.*

Ground Rules and Introductions (10 minutes)

Establish the four ground rules clearly. You can post them on a flipchart or simply state them. Either way, name each one and pause briefly between them so participants can absorb.

> *Before we go any further, I want to lay down four ground rules that hold up everything we will do together over the next six weeks.*

1. **What is shared in this room stays in this room.** Names, stories, situations — they belong only to the people in the room. Confidentiality is not optional.
2. **You are never required to share.** If I ask a question and you would rather not answer it, you can pass without explanation. We will not pressure anyone.
3. **We are not here to fix each other.** If someone shares something hard, our job is to listen, not to give advice. Most of us already get plenty of unsolicited advice in our lives. We will try not to add to it.
4. **We use respectful language.** People grieve differently. People believe different things. People come from different kinds of families. We are not here to judge any of that.

Now invite introductions.

> *I want to go around the room. When it is your turn, please share your first name and one sentence — just one sentence — about what brought you here. There is no wrong answer. You can be specific or general. You can be light or serious. Just one sentence.*

Model it yourself first. Then go around. Listen carefully. If someone shares something heavy, simply say, "Thank you for sharing that," and move on. Do not pause to address every participant's sentence in detail. The goal of this segment is for everyone to hear their own voice in the room and to hear the voices of the others. That is enough.

App Onboarding Together (8 minutes)

This segment is one of the most important things you will do in the entire course. Walking participants through downloading the Life Now & Beyond app together – in the room, with you guiding them – dramatically increases the chance that they will actually use the app over the next six weeks. The app is woven into every module that follows. Participants who leave Module 1 with the app installed and a free account set up are participants who will get the most from this course.

Make sure participants have their phones out. If anyone forgot their phone, pair them with someone who can show them the app on screen during this segment, and make a note to help them download between sessions.

> *Now I want us to do something together. Please pull out your phones. We are going to take about 8 minutes to get the Life Now & Beyond app installed on your phones, set up free accounts, and take a quick tour. The app is the digital companion to this course. We will use it almost every week, and the work you do in it will continue to be useful long after the course is over.*

Step one. Open your phone's app store. That is the App Store on iPhone or the Google Play Store on Android. Search for *Life Now and Beyond.* The app icon is the Life Now and Beyond logo. Tap to download. While that is installing, the rest of you who already have it installed, please open it.

Wait until everyone has the app installed. Help anyone having trouble. This is normal. Some people will be slower than others, and that is fine. *The group will wait.*

Now, set up a free account. The app will walk you through this. You will create an account with your email or sign in with Apple or Google. The free tier gives you everything we need for the early weeks of the course. There is also a premium tier, which we will talk about later in the course – not tonight. Tonight is just about getting started.

Wait again until everyone has an account. *Be patient. This is the most important investment of time in the entire first session.*

Now give a quick tour. On the home screen there are two main paths: **Before Someone Passes Away** and **After Someone Has Passed Away**. The course will move through both over six weeks. **Trusted Access** sits at the top – you will talk about it in week four. The bottom tabs are *Home, Journal, Binder, Resources, Settings.* The Resources tab holds articles and books. The Binder tab is where participants will organize their own information.

Send participants home with a small task: spend ten minutes exploring on their own and read "The Conversation We All Avoid" in the Resources tab before next week. Then bring the room back to focus. Phones away or face-down. Begin the main teaching segment.

Teaching Segment: The Conversation We Avoid (15 minutes)

This is the main teaching content. The goal is to help participants see, with fresh eyes, the strangeness of how our culture handles death — and the personal cost of going along with that avoidance.

> "*I want to start with a simple observation. We are all going to die. Every single person in this room. Every person in our families. Every person we love. There is no exception. And yet, we live in a culture that treats this fact as if it were optional. We treat it as if mentioning it is rude. We treat it as if making any preparation for it is morbid. And the result is that almost no one is ready when it happens.*

Pause and let that land.

> "*Think about how strange that is. We prepare for almost everything else. We buy insurance for cars we might never crash. We plan vacations months in advance. We save for retirements that may or may not happen. But the one event that is absolutely guaranteed to happen — to us, and to everyone we love — we treat as if planning for it is bad luck.*

Offer the three reasons. List them on the board if you have one.

First, we live in a culture that has hidden death. A hundred and fifty years ago, most people died at home, surrounded by family. Today, most people die in hospitals or facilities. Bodies are removed by professionals. Funerals last an hour. We have outsourced death to specialists, and in doing so, we have forgotten how to face it ourselves.

Second, we are afraid that talking about death will somehow cause it. There is a superstition many of us carry without realizing it: *if I write a will, I will die soon. If I plan my funeral, I am inviting it. If I ask my parents about their wishes, I am wishing them away.* None of that is true. Writing a will does not kill anyone. But the fear is real, and it stops us.

Third, we love the people in our lives, and the thought of losing them is so painful that we would rather not look at it. So we change the subject. We say, "Let us not talk about that now." And eventually, the conversation we needed to have is the one we never had, because the person we needed to have it with is gone.

Now pivot to the cost.

> *Here is the cost. When we do not have these conversations, the people we love pay for it. They pay for it in confusion. They pay for it in conflict. They pay for it in money. They pay for it in months of unnecessary stress while they sort through what we left behind.*

Alice Truman, the author of the books this course is built around, tells the story of her own mother's death. Her mother left behind three filing cabinets, a safety deposit box no one knew about, and a handwritten note that said, "Burial or cremation, I cannot decide." Alice and her siblings spent six months sorting through paperwork and trying to guess what their mother would have wanted. They found insurance policies that had lapsed. Bank accounts no one knew existed. In the middle of their grief, they had to be detectives.

> *That is the cost of avoidance. Not for the person who died. For the people left behind.*

Offer the alternative.

There is another way. Some families do this differently. They have the conversations. They make the plans. They organize the documents. And when death comes — because it will come — those families gather peacefully. They grieve without drowning in logistics. They know what their loved one wanted. **That is the difference between chaos and clarity. And the difference is preparation.**

That is what this course is going to help you do, in two directions. We are going to help you prepare for losses you may face — losses of people you love. And we are going to help you prepare your own affairs, so the people who love you do not inherit a mess. Six weeks from now, you will not be done. This work does not finish. But you will have started, and you will know how to keep going.

Discussion (15 minutes)

Choose two or three of the following questions. Read the room and pick the ones that fit your group. Begin with the lighter questions; move to the deeper ones if the group is ready.

- What is one thing about death or grief that no one in your family ever talked about when you were growing up?
- Has there been a death in your life — distant or close — where the lack of preparation made things harder than they needed to be?
- Has there been a death in your life where someone did the preparation, and it made a real difference?
- What is one conversation you have been meaning to have with someone in your family but have not had yet? What has stopped you?
- When you imagine your own death, what is the part you most want your family to know in advance?

- What did you hope to get out of this course when you signed up?

A NOTE FOR THE TEACHER DURING DISCUSSION

Your most important job during discussion is to listen and to give space.

When someone shares something hard, do not rush to comment. A slow nod, a soft "thank you," and a moment of silence are often more honoring than words.

If one person is dominating, gently turn to others: "I want to make sure others have a chance to weigh in. What about the rest of you?"

If the group is silent, do not panic. Wait. Silence is sometimes the sound of people thinking. If silence stretches past 20 seconds, rephrase the question or offer a personal reflection of your own.

In-Class Activity: Why I Am Here (5 minutes)

Distribute Handout 1B. Give participants three minutes to write privately. Then invite anyone who wishes to share a sentence or two from what they wrote.

> *I am giving each of you a handout titled "Why I Am Here." Take three minutes to fill it out privately. There is no right or wrong answer. After three minutes, I will invite anyone who wishes to share a sentence or two, but no one is required to.*

After three minutes, invite sharing. Let two or three voices speak. Then move to closing.

Closing and Preview of Module 2 (5 minutes)

Distribute Handout 1C with reading assignments and reflection prompts. Preview what is coming.

> *Before we close, let me tell you what is coming next week. In Module 2, we are going to start the practical work. We will talk about wills and trusts, healthcare directives, financial documents, and funeral planning.*

The goal of next week is not to make you an expert. The goal is to help you see what needs to exist, what needs to be where, and what needs to be communicated to the people who will need it someday. The reading is on the handout I just gave you. The handout also has two short reflection questions. Please give them a few minutes between now and next week.

> *Thank you each of you for being here tonight. This is hard material. You showed up. That is not small. I will see you next week.*

End on time. Allow participants to linger if they wish. Be available for anyone who wants a brief private word, but do not initiate conversations beyond a warm goodbye.

Reading Assignments for Next Week

If your participants have *When a Loved One Dies*: Parallel reading: Chapter 4 (Essential Documents and Accounts). This chapter shows what happens with documents after a death. Reading it gives participants the "why" behind next week's preparation work.

If your participants have *Not My Favorite Subject Either, But...*: Primary reading: Chapters 3, 4, 5, and 6 (Legal Must-Haves, Money Matters, Health and End-of-Life Choices, Funeral and Memorial Planning). This is a substantial reading load. Encourage participants to skim what is overwhelming and read closely what catches their attention. They are not expected to absorb every detail in one week.

If your participants have both books: Read the primary chapters from *Not My Favorite Subject Either, But...*, and skim Chapter 4 of *When a Loved One Dies* for context.

App Integration

Because we did app onboarding together in class, every participant should leave Module 1 with the Life Now & Beyond app installed and a free account set up. The between-session activity is light: explore the app on their own and read one article from the Resource hub.

> **THIS WEEK, IN THE APP**
> You already have the app installed and your account set up — we did that together. This week, just spend ten minutes on your own exploring. Look around the Home Dashboard, the Resources tab, and the Binder tab. There is an article called "*The Conversation We All Avoid*" in the Resources tab that picks up where we left off tonight — please read it before next week. If you feel ready, the Before Journey has a first chapter called "*Who You Are*" that you can begin. Everything we are doing this week is in the free tier.

Sensitivity Notes

Recent Loss in the Room

Some of your participants may be in fresh grief. The early discussion can stir powerful emotions, even when the questions seem general. If a participant becomes visibly upset during introductions or discussion, do not abandon the rest of the group to focus on them, but offer a quiet acknowledgment in the moment ("Take your time," or "We are with you,") and check in with that participant briefly after the session.

Reluctant Participants

Occasionally, a participant attends because someone else encouraged them. They may be visibly uncomfortable or skeptical. Do not single them out. Do not pressure them to speak. Often, by Module 3 or 4, these participants become some of the most engaged people in the room. Trust the process.

The "I Already Know All This" Participant

Some participants — especially those with a professional background in law, finance, healthcare, or funeral services — may indicate that they are already familiar with the material. Honor their experience without letting it dominate the room. A useful response: "Wonderful. Your perspective will be valuable to others in this group. I may call on you when we hit your area of expertise."

Cultural and Religious Differences

Your group will likely include people from different cultural and religious backgrounds. Be especially attentive in this first session to how different participants describe family customs, funeral traditions, and beliefs about what happens after death. Treat all of these as valid. The course does not promote any particular view.

NOTES

REPRODUCIBLE HANDOUTS

Module 1

The following pages may be photocopied for classroom use.
Each handout is designed to fit a single 8.5 × 11 page.

HANDOUT 1A
Welcome and Course Overview
REPRODUCIBLE HANDOUT

Welcome to **Life Now and Beyond**, a six-week course on preparing for, facing, and healing from the death of a loved one. Over the next six weeks, you will explore both halves of how families handle death: the preparation that happens before a loss, and the practical and emotional journey that follows it.

What to Expect Each Week

Each session is approximately one hour. You will receive reading assignments to complete between sessions and a short reflection or activity to bring with you. Participation in discussion is invited but never required.

The Six Modules

- **Module 1** · The Conversation We Avoid
- **Module 2** · Getting Your Affairs in Order
- **Module 3** · The Immediate Aftermath
- **Module 4** · Documents, Legal Matters, and Digital Life
- **Module 5** · Grief, Family, and Self-Care
- **Module 6** · Moving Forward and Leaving a Legacy

The Books

This course is built around two books by Alice Truman: *When a Loved One Dies* and *Not My Favorite Subject Either, But...* You will get the most from this course by reading the assigned chapters between sessions.

The Companion App

Visit **lifenowandbeyond.com** to access the digital companion to your books. The app provides interactive checklists, planning tools, and resources you can use throughout this course and well beyond it.

Group Ground Rules

1. What is shared here stays here.
2. You are never required to share.
3. We are not here to fix each other.
4. We use respectful language.

HANDOUT 1B

Why I Am Here

REPRODUCIBLE HANDOUT

Take three minutes to write your honest answers to the questions below. This handout is for you. You may share parts of it with the group if you wish, but you are not required to.

1. What brought me to this course?

2. What is one specific loss, conversation, or decision I am thinking about as I begin this course?

3. What would it mean for me to feel more ready six weeks from now?

4. What do I most need from this group in order to do this work?

HANDOUT 1C

Reading and Reflection for Week 2

REPRODUCIBLE HANDOUT

Reading

If you have *Not My Favorite Subject Either, But...* read Chapters 3 through 6 (Legal Must-Haves, Money Matters, Health and End-of-Life Choices, Funeral and Memorial Planning). Skim what feels overwhelming. Read closely what catches your attention.

If you have *When a Loved One Dies* read Chapter 4 (Essential Documents and Accounts) for context on what happens with documents after a death.

If you have both books, read the primary chapters from *Not My Favorite Subject Either, But...*, and skim Chapter 4 of *When a Loved One Dies.*

Reflection Questions

Spend a few minutes between now and next session thinking about each question. Bring this page with you next week.

1. Of the four areas you will read about (legal, money, health, funeral), which one have you done the most about? Which have you done the least about?

2. If something happened to you in the next year, who in your life would have the hardest time figuring out what to do? Why?

App Activity

You set up your Life Now & Beyond account in class. This week, spend ten minutes exploring the app on your own. Read "*The Conversation We All Avoid*" in the Resources tab. Optional: begin Chapter 1 of the Before Journey ("Who You Are").

WEEK TWO

MODULE

02

Getting Your Affairs in Order

The four pillars that turn chaos into clarity.

Module Overview

Module 2 is the practical heart of the preparation half of the course. Over one session, participants will get an honest, organized look at the four major areas that everyone needs to address before they die: the legal documents, the financial picture, the healthcare and end-of-life choices, and the funeral and memorial preferences. The goal is not to complete any of these areas tonight. The goal is for every participant to leave with a clear map of what needs to exist, what they have already done, and what still needs attention.

This module will feel different from Module 1. Where Module 1 was about feelings, framing, and motivation, Module 2 is about logistics. Many participants will find this reassuring. Others may feel overwhelmed by the volume of material. Your job is to keep the tone steady and the message simple: *nobody finishes this work in one week, and starting somewhere is more important than starting everywhere.*

Learning Objectives

By the end of Module 2, participants will be able to:

- Name the core legal documents every adult should have, including a will, a power of attorney, and an advance healthcare directive
- Describe the difference between a will and a trust at a basic level and recognize when professional legal help is needed
- Identify what a complete personal financial inventory should include
- Articulate at least two healthcare or end-of-life choices that they would want documented
- List the major funeral and memorial decisions that families face, and recognize the value of documenting their own preferences in advance

Materials Needed

- Teacher's Guide
- Sign-in sheet
- Tissues, water
- Reproducible Handout 2A: The Four Pillars of Preparation
- Reproducible Handout 2B: My Affairs Self-Assessment
- Reproducible Handout 2C: Reading and Reflection for Week 3
- A whiteboard or flipchart for capturing group input (optional)

Lesson Plan with Timing

Recommended session length: 60 minutes. Plan for 60 to 90 minutes to allow for natural discussion.

TIME	SEGMENT	PURPOSE
0:00 – 0:05	**Welcome and Reconnection**	Brief check-in on how the past week landed. Acknowledge that the reading was substantial.
0:05 – 0:35	**Teaching Segment: The Four Pillars**	Walk through legal, financial, healthcare, and funeral preparation. Use Handout 2A.
0:35 – 0:50	**Self-Assessment Activity**	Participants complete Handout 2B privately. Brief sharing in pairs or small groups. *Flex point — extend by 5 to 10 minutes if useful.*
0:50 – 0:57	**Discussion**	Open discussion drawing on the self-assessment.
0:57 – 1:00	**Closing and Preview of Module 3**	Distribute reading assignments. Preview what is coming.

Teacher's Script and Talking Points

Welcome and Reconnection (5 minutes)

> *"Welcome back. I hope this week was alright. The reading I gave you last week was substantial — four chapters — and I do not expect that anyone read every word. That is fine. The point of the reading was to introduce you to the territory, not to make you an expert in it. Tonight we are going to walk through that territory together.*

Briefly invite check-in. "*Anything from the reading that surprised you? Anything that hit hard? You do not have to share, but if something is sitting with you, this is a good moment for it.*" Keep this short — two or three minutes max. The substance of tonight is the teaching segment.

Teaching Segment: The Four Pillars of Preparation (30 minutes)

This segment walks through the four major areas every adult needs to address. Use Handout 2A as your visual companion. Aim for about 7 minutes per pillar, leaving a couple of minutes for transitions.

Pillar 1: Legal

The first pillar is legal. There are three documents every adult should have, regardless of age, regardless of how much money they have, regardless of whether they have children.

The first is a will. A will is a legal document that says what happens to your stuff after you die and, if you have minor children, who takes care of them. If you do not have a will when you die, the state where you live decides those things for you. The state's decisions are usually fine for simple situations and often a disaster for complicated ones. A will is not expensive. It is not difficult. The vast majority of adults should have one.

The second is a durable power of attorney. This document names someone to make financial and legal decisions for you if you become unable to make them yourself. Without it, your family may have to go to court to get permission to pay your bills or manage your accounts while you are still alive but incapacitated. That is an avoidable disaster.

The third is an advance healthcare directive, sometimes called a living will or a healthcare power of attorney. This document does two things: it states your wishes about medical treatment in end-of-life situations, and it names someone to make medical decisions for you if you cannot. Without this document, your family may be forced to make life-and-death choices for you with no idea what you would have wanted.

Some people also need a **trust**. A trust is a more complex tool that lets you transfer assets without going through the probate court process. Whether you need one depends on your assets, your family situation, and the laws in your state. This is a question for an estate planning attorney, not a question this course can answer for you.

A NOTE ON DOING THIS YOURSELF

Online forms can produce valid documents in many states for simple situations. They can also produce documents that are useless, invalid, or accidentally damaging in complicated situations. If your situation is simple — a single person, modest assets, no minor children, no business, no estranged relatives — a reputable online tool may serve you. *If your situation is more complex than that, hire an attorney.*

Pillar 2: Financial

The second pillar is financial. The goal here is not to manage your money differently. The goal is to make sure that **someone other than you knows where your money is.**

A complete financial inventory includes: bank accounts and where they are, retirement accounts and how to access them, life insurance policies and where the documents live, real estate and any mortgages on it, investments and the account numbers, debts of any kind and who they are owed to, recurring bills and how they are paid, safe deposit boxes and who has access, and any digital financial accounts including cryptocurrency.

The mistake most people make is not financial. It is informational. They have all of this stuff scattered across drawers, online accounts, paper files, and their own memories. When they die, their families have to reconstruct it from scratch — which is exactly what Alice Truman and her siblings had to do after her mother died. *That is what we are trying to spare our families.*

A simple solution is what Alice calls a **"final binder"** or what some people call a "when I die" file. It is a single physical or digital location where everything is documented. We will go deeper on the final binder in Module 4.

Pillar 3: Healthcare and End-of-Life Choices

The third pillar is healthcare. We have already mentioned the advance healthcare directive. But there is more to this pillar than the document itself. There is the conversation behind it.

The directive asks you to think about questions most of us avoid: *If I am in a permanent coma, do I want to be kept alive on machines? If I have advanced dementia and stop eating, do I want to be fed through a tube? If my heart stops in a situation where CPR might bring me back but might also leave me with severe brain damage, do I want CPR?* These are not abstract questions. These are the actual questions someone will eventually be asked about you, by a doctor, in a hospital corridor.

You can leave those decisions to your family. Many people do. But it is a heavy gift to leave them. Spouses and adult children who have to make those calls without knowing what their loved one would have wanted carry that weight for years.

Two other tools matter here. A **POLST** or **MOLST** form, depending on your state, is a medical order signed by a physician that travels with you and tells emergency responders what level of intervention you want. It is appropriate for people with serious illnesses. A **do-not-resuscitate** order, or DNR, is similar and is also for people with serious illnesses or advanced age. If you are healthy, you do not need either of these yet — the advance directive is what matters. If you have a serious diagnosis, talk to your doctor.

Pillar 4: Funeral and Memorial Preferences

The fourth pillar is funeral and memorial planning. Most people who have lost a loved one will tell you that the funeral planning was one of the worst parts of the experience — not because of grief, but because they had to make a dozen significant decisions, with significant costs attached, in the first 48 hours after the death, while in shock.

You can spare your family from this. The decisions are not difficult to think about in advance. They are: *Burial or cremation? If burial, where, and have you purchased a plot? If cremation, what should be done with the remains? What kind of service do you want, if any? Religious or secular? Where? Who should officiate? Are there specific readings or music you want? Who would you want to speak? What should the obituary say? Are there charities you would want donations directed to instead of flowers?*

You can write down your answers to all of these questions tonight, in an evening, and your family will be infinitely grateful. Or you can leave it to them at the worst possible moment in their lives. **The choice you make about this is one of the kindest or the cruelest decisions you will ever make about your own death.**

> **A WORD ABOUT OVERWHELM**
> This is a lot. If you are sitting there thinking, "I have not done any of this and I have no idea where to start," that is normal. Most adults are in exactly that position. The point of this course is not to make you feel bad about where you are. The point is to give you a starting place. We are about to do an exercise that will help you see, on one page, where you stand on each of these four pillars. From there, you will know what your next step is. *You do not need to do everything. You need to do the next thing.*

Self-Assessment Activity (15 minutes)

Distribute Handout 2B. Give participants 8 to 10 minutes to fill it out privately. Then have them turn to a neighbor and share whatever they are comfortable sharing for about 5 minutes. Make clear that nothing on the handout has to be shared with the larger group.

> *I am giving each of you a handout called "My Affairs Self-Assessment." Take about 8 minutes to fill it out privately. Be honest. Nobody is going to grade this. After 8 minutes, I will ask you to turn to the person next to you and share whatever you are comfortable sharing for a few minutes. You do not have to share specifics. You can just say where you feel strong and where you feel behind.*

After the pair sharing, bring the room back together.

Discussion (7 minutes)

Open discussion. Choose one or two questions.

- Which of the four pillars feels most overwhelming to you, and why?
- Was there anything on the self-assessment that surprised you — either how much you have done or how little?
- Has anyone in your family already done some of this work? What did they do, and how did you find out?
- What is one specific thing you want to do this week to make progress on one of the four pillars?

Closing and Preview of Module 3 (3 minutes)

> *"Next week we shift gears. Modules 1 and 2 have been about preparation – about getting ready, about doing the work in advance. Module 3 is about what happens when a death occurs. We will walk through the first 24 hours, the next 72 hours, and the planning of services. This is the territory of When a Loved One Dies, and the reading is from Chapters 1, 2, and 3 of that book.*

Some of you in this room have lived through this already. Some of you have not, and may not for many years. Either way, the next module gives you a clear, step-by-step understanding of what happens, so that whenever it does come, you are not facing it for the first time. Thank you for tonight. I will see you next week.

Reading Assignments for Next Week

If your participants have *When a Loved One Dies***:** No primary reading this week from this book.

If your participants have *Not My Favorite Subject Either, But...***:** No primary reading; participants are completing the four-chapter assignment from last week if not finished.

If your participants have both books: Read Chapters 1, 2, and 3 of *When a Loved One Dies* (The First 24 Hours, The Next 72 Hours, Preparing for Services). Skim Chapter 6 of *Not My Favorite Subject Either, But...* (Funeral and Memorial Planning) as parallel reading.

App Integration

The four pillars of preparation map directly onto sections of the app's Life Binder. Two of the pillars (Medical and the Final Wishes part of Funeral Planning) live in free Life Binder sections, as does Personal Information. The Legal Documents, Financial Information, and Insurance Policies sections are premium. Free participants can do meaningful work tonight on Personal Information, Medical Information, and Final Wishes; Legal and Financial will require either premium or paper-based work for now.

> **THIS WEEK, IN THE APP**
>
> In the Life Now & Beyond app, open the Life Binder. You will see seven sections, three of which are free: Personal Information, Medical Information, and Final Wishes. Spend 20 minutes filling in what you can in those three sections. The Insurance, Financial, Legal, and Digital Legacy sections will show as premium – you can come back to those later. You can also begin Before Journey Chapters 2 through 5 (Your Health, Your Coverage, Your Finances, Your Wishes in Writing). The Before Journey is fully free.

Sensitivity Notes

The "I Have Not Done Any of This" Participant

Many participants will leave this module feeling behind, behind, behind. Watch for signs of overwhelm: a participant going quiet, someone making self-deprecating jokes, someone trying to brush off the material as not applicable to them. Reinforce often that nobody finishes this work in one week, that almost no adults are fully prepared, and that the goal is to take the next step, not to do everything.

The "I Have Done All of This" Participant

Some participants will arrive having done significant preparation. They are at risk of dominating the conversation or, alternately, feeling that the module is not for them. Honor what they have done. Invite them to share what worked, what they wish they had known earlier, and what they are still working on. Even the most prepared people typically have gaps.

Real Decisions in Real Time

Some participants will be wrestling with these exact questions for an aging parent or seriously ill spouse. The teaching content can hit very close to home. If a participant becomes emotional, do not redirect away from the content — simply slow down, acknowledge ("This is real for you right now, isn't it"), and continue at a pace that honors what is happening in the room.

Refer, Refer, Refer

This is the module where the temptation to give specific legal, financial, or medical advice is highest. Resist it. Use the language: "That is a great question for an attorney who knows your state. The course can point you toward what to ask. It cannot give you the answer."

NOTES

REPRODUCIBLE HANDOUTS

Module 2

The following pages may be photocopied for classroom use.
Each handout is designed to fit a single 8.5 × 11 page.

HANDOUT 2A

The Four Pillars of Preparation

REPRODUCIBLE HANDOUT

Every adult needs to address four major areas in order to leave their affairs in order. Use this handout as a reference during and after tonight's session.

Pillar 1: Legal

- Will (every adult should have one)
- Durable Power of Attorney for finances
- Advance Healthcare Directive (also called a living will or healthcare power of attorney)
- Trust (depending on assets and family situation — ask an attorney)

Pillar 2: Financial

- Bank and retirement accounts inventoried in one location
- Life insurance policies and where they are filed
- Real estate, mortgages, debts, recurring bills documented
- Safe deposit box location and access
- Digital financial accounts including cryptocurrency

Pillar 3: Healthcare and End-of-Life Choices

- Advance Healthcare Directive completed and shared with family and physicians
- Healthcare proxy or agent named
- Specific wishes documented (life support, feeding tubes, CPR, comfort care)
- POLST or MOLST and DNR (if applicable, with physician's guidance)

Pillar 4: Funeral and Memorial Preferences

- Burial vs. cremation
- Cemetery plot or cremation disposition wishes
- Type of service (religious, secular, none)
- Officiant, location, music, readings, speakers
- Obituary preferences and donations in lieu of flowers
- Pre-payment or pre-arrangements (only if you trust the provider)

WHEN TO HIRE A PROFESSIONAL

Always for trusts, complex estates, blended families, business ownership, and any situation involving significant assets or potential family conflict. **Often** for wills and powers of attorney depending on your state and complexity. **Always** for medical orders like POLST and DNR. The cost of professional help is almost always less than the cost of getting it wrong.

HANDOUT 2B

My Affairs Self-Assessment

REPRODUCIBLE HANDOUT

Mark each item honestly. This handout is for you. You will not be asked to share specifics with the group.

Legal

I have a current will: Yes No Outdated

I have a Durable Power of Attorney: Yes No Not sure

I have an Advance Healthcare Directive: Yes No Not sure

I know whether I need a trust: Yes No

Financial

Someone other than me knows where my bank accounts are: Yes Partially No

My life insurance policies are findable: Yes No I do not have life insurance

My recurring bills and debts are documented somewhere: Yes Partially No

I have started a "final binder" or equivalent: Yes In progress No

Healthcare

My family knows my wishes about life support: Yes Partially No

I have named a healthcare agent in writing: Yes No

My healthcare directive is on file with my doctor: Yes No Not sure

Funeral

I have decided burial or cremation: Yes No

My family knows what kind of service I want: Yes Partially No

I have written down any specific funeral or memorial wishes: Yes No

Reflection

Looking at the boxes I checked, where am I strongest?

Where am I weakest?

What is one specific thing I will do this week?

HANDOUT 2C

Reading and Reflection for Week 3

REPRODUCIBLE HANDOUT

Reading

If you have *When a Loved One Dies*, read Chapters 1, 2, and 3 (The First 24 Hours, The Next 72 Hours, Preparing for Services).

If you have *Not My Favorite Subject Either, But...*, review Chapter 6 (Funeral and Memorial Planning) if you have not already read it in detail.

If you have both books, read the primary chapters from *When a Loved One Dies* and use the funeral planning chapter from *Not My Favorite Subject Either, But...* as parallel reading.

Reflection Questions

1. Have you ever been the person who had to make decisions in the first 24 to 72 hours after a death? If so, what was the hardest part?

2. If a death happened in your immediate family this weekend, who would step up to handle the practical decisions? Is that the right person? Do they know they would be it?

App Activity

In the Life Now & Beyond app, open the Life Binder. Spend 20 minutes filling in what you can in the three free sections: Personal Information, Medical Information, and Final Wishes. The Insurance, Financial, Legal, and Digital Legacy sections will appear as premium. Begin Before Journey Chapters 2 through 5 (Your Health, Your Coverage, Your Finances, Your Wishes in Writing) at your own pace. *The Before Journey is fully free.*

WEEK THREE

MODULE

03

The Immediate Aftermath

The first 24 hours, the next 72, and the planning of services.

Module Overview

Module 3 is the practical heart of the aftermath half of the course. Tonight, participants will walk through what happens — step by step, hour by hour — in the time immediately after a loved one dies. The first 24 hours. The next 72 hours. The first major task: planning a funeral or memorial service.

This is a module where participants who have been through this before may find old wounds reopening. It is also a module where participants who have not been through this find themselves understanding, perhaps for the first time, what their family members went through after a death years ago. Plan for both responses to be in the room.

The goal of this module is twofold: to give participants who may face this in the near future a clear roadmap, and to honor those who have already walked this road by validating how hard it was.

Learning Objectives

By the end of Module 3, participants will be able to:

- Describe the essential steps in the first 24 hours after a death, including obtaining a legal pronouncement and notifying immediate family
- Identify the major decisions that arise in the next 72 hours, including selecting a funeral home and beginning service planning
- List the core decisions involved in planning a funeral or memorial service
- Articulate what they would want their own family to do in the first 72 hours after their death
- Recognize the value of designating, in advance, who will handle these decisions

Materials Needed

- Teacher's Guide
- Sign-in sheet, tissues, water
- Reproducible Handout 3A: The First 72 Hours at a Glance
- Reproducible Handout 3B: Funeral and Memorial Decisions Worksheet
- Reproducible Handout 3C: Reading and Reflection for Week 4

Lesson Plan with Timing

Recommended session length: 60 minutes. Plan for 60 to 90 minutes to allow for natural discussion. *This module often runs long because participants share stories of their own losses.*

TIME	SEGMENT	PURPOSE
0:00 – 0:05	**Welcome and Reconnection**	Brief check-in. Acknowledge that tonight's material is heavy.
0:05 – 0:20	**Teaching Segment: The First 24 Hours**	Walk through the essential steps.
0:20 – 0:35	**The Next 72 Hours and Service Planning**	Walk through the next stage and the major service decisions.
0:35 – 0:50	**Activity and Discussion**	Participants begin Handout 3B. Open discussion. *Flex point — extend by 5 to 10 minutes.*
0:50 – 0:57	**Stories from the Group**	Invite anyone who wishes to share something from their own experience.
0:57 – 1:00	**Closing and Preview of Module 4**	Distribute reading. Close warmly.

Teacher's Script and Talking Points

Welcome and Reconnection (5 minutes)

> *"Welcome back. Tonight we shift from preparation to aftermath. We are going to walk through what actually happens in the first 24 hours, the next 72 hours, and the planning of services after a loved one dies. Some of you have lived through this. Some of you have not. Either way, tonight is meant to give you a clear understanding of what unfolds, so the territory is no longer unfamiliar.*

I want to say at the start: *if at any point tonight feels like too much, it is okay to step out for a few minutes. We will be here when you come back.*

Teaching Segment: The First 24 Hours (15 minutes)

When someone dies, the first 24 hours are often a blur. People describe feeling numb, in shock, as if they are watching themselves move through the world. That is normal. The body and the mind protect us in those first hours. *You do not have to feel sharp.* You have to take a few essential steps, and then you can rest.

There are six things that need to happen in the first 24 hours.

1. **Get a legal pronouncement of death.** If your loved one dies at home, you call 911. If hospice is involved, the hospice nurse can usually handle this without 911. If your loved one dies in a hospital or care facility, the staff handles it. *Why this matters*: until a death is legally pronounced, nothing else can move forward. You will need that pronouncement to obtain death certificates, which you will need for almost everything that follows.
2. **Notify immediate family.** Spouse, children, parents, siblings. This can be overwhelming when you are in shock. Choose one or two people to help you. Ask them to call extended family and close friends so you do not have to make every call yourself. There is no rule that says you must post on social media right away. Wait until you are ready.
3. **Arrange care for dependents and pets.** If your loved one was caring for children, an elderly parent, or animals, make sure they are safe and looked after. This does not have to be a permanent arrangement — it just has to cover the next day or two while you find your footing.
4. **Select a funeral home, at least temporarily.** If your loved one died at home, in a hospital, or in a care facility, the body needs to be transported. The hospital or hospice will ask which funeral home to call. You can change funeral homes later if you decide to. If your loved one had a prearranged funeral plan, locate that paperwork now. And know that funeral homes are required by federal law to give you a price list. **You have the right to compare prices. You are not obligated to buy the most expensive option.**
5. **Secure the home.** Lock the doors. Take care of the mail. Water the plants. Check on pets and livestock. This sounds practical because it is, and it is also the kind of thing that gets forgotten in the fog. If you cannot face going to your loved one's home, ask someone you trust to do it.
6. **Take care of yourself.** Drink water. Eat something. Rest. Accept help when it is offered. *You do not have to do everything today. You will not be able to do everything today.*

The Next 72 Hours and Service Planning (15 minutes)

Once the first day is behind you, the fog usually lifts just enough to take a few more steps. The next 72 hours are about laying the groundwork for the arrangements ahead.

You will need some **documents**: birth certificate, Social Security card, marriage certificate if applicable, military discharge papers if your loved one was a veteran, insurance policies, any will or trust paperwork. If you cannot find everything immediately, do not panic. Just start a folder or a box where everything can be collected.

You will also begin **notifications**: the employer, if your loved one was working, who can tell you about pay, benefits, and any life insurance. Religious or cultural leaders, if a faith-based service is desired. Close friends and community members, which can be delegated.

And you will **meet with a funeral director**. This is when funeral planning begins in earnest. The funeral director will walk you through the major decisions. There are roughly seven of them.

1. **Burial or cremation.** This is often the biggest decision and may already be answered by your loved one's wishes or by family or religious tradition. If your loved one prepaid for arrangements, those plans take care of much of this.
2. **The type of service.** Traditional funeral with a viewing? Memorial service without the body present? Graveside only? A celebration of life? No service at all?
3. **The location.** Funeral home, religious building, cemetery, private home, or somewhere meaningful to your loved one.
4. **The details.** Who will officiate? What music? What readings? Will there be eulogies, and from whom? Will children attend? Will there be food?
5. **Practical considerations.** Casket or urn selection, flowers, transportation, programs.
6. **Written materials.** The obituary. The order of service. Any printed memorial item.
7. **Final coordination.** The timing, the guest list, any reception afterward, communicating all of it to the people who need to know.

THE MOST IMPORTANT TAKEAWAY

Every one of these decisions is easier when the deceased person made their preferences known in advance. **Every one.** This is why Module 2 mattered. The work you do for yourself — deciding burial or cremation, choosing music, writing your obituary — is a gift you give the people you love. They will not have to guess. They will not have to argue. They will simply do what you asked.

Activity and Discussion (15 minutes)

Distribute Handout 3B. Have participants begin filling out the first half (their own funeral and memorial preferences). After 8 minutes, open discussion.

> *I am giving you a worksheet titled "Funeral and Memorial Decisions." Take 8 minutes to start filling it out. This is for you and your future family. Many of these questions you will not have answered before. That is fine. The exercise of considering them is the point.*

After 8 minutes, open discussion.

- Which of these decisions is hardest for you to think about for yourself?
- Are there any decisions on this list where you already have strong preferences? What are they, and do the people who would handle your funeral know?

- For those who have planned a funeral for a loved one, what was harder than you expected? What was easier?

Stories from the Group (7 minutes)

Invite anyone who wishes to share a brief story. Frame it carefully:

> *Some of you have walked this road already. If you would be willing to share something from your own experience — something that helped, something that was hard, something you wish you had known — that gift can mean a lot to others in the room who have not yet had to do this.*

Let two or three voices speak. Honor each story with a "Thank you for sharing that." Do not commentate.

Closing and Preview of Module 4 (3 minutes)

> *Next week we move into the paperwork. Documents, legal matters, and digital life. After a death, there is a long list of accounts to close, agencies to notify, and paperwork to complete. We will walk through it. The reading is from Chapters 4, 5, and 6 of When a Loved One Dies, and Chapters 7, 8, and 9 of Not My Favorite Subject Either, But... — again, you do not have to read every word, but skim widely. Thank you for tonight. I will see you next week.*

Reading Assignments for Next Week

If your participants have *When a Loved One Dies***:** Primary reading: Chapters 4, 5, and 6 (Essential Documents and Accounts, Legal Matters, Digital Life).

If your participants have *Not My Favorite Subject Either, But...***:** Parallel reading: Chapters 7, 8, and 9 (Digital Afterlife, Personal Legacy Projects, Organizing the "Final Binder").

If your participants have both books: Read the primary chapters from *When a Loved One Dies* and the parallel chapters from *Not My Favorite Subject Either, But...* Together they cover both sides of the same territory.

App Integration

The Resource hub of the Life Now & Beyond app contains three free articles that cover tonight's territory: "*The First 24 Hours*," "*The Next 72 Hours*," and "*Preparing for Services*." These are substantive articles. The deeper After-Loss Guidance & Support workspace is a 22-step interactive premium feature. Participants who want to see what it looks like can preview it from the home screen.

> **THIS WEEK, IN THE APP**
> Read at least one of the three articles in the Resource hub: "*The First 24 Hours*," "*The Next 72 Hours*," or "*Preparing for Services*." These are free. The After-Loss workspace organizes everything into a 22-step tool — that is premium, but you can preview it from the home screen.

Sensitivity Notes

Re-Triggered Grief

This module reactivates grief for participants who have lost loved ones. Even years-old losses can feel fresh tonight. Watch for participants who become quieter than usual, who tear up unexpectedly, or who seem far away. Acknowledge gently after the session: "Tonight's material was a lot. How are you doing?"

Anticipatory Grief

Participants caring for a seriously ill or aging loved one may be sitting with the awareness that they will be doing this themselves in the near future. The teaching content can feel personal in a way it does not for everyone. Honor the weight of this without trying to lift it.

When Stories Get Heavy

In the "Stories from the Group" segment, occasionally a participant will share something extraordinarily painful: a sudden death, a child's death, a death involving violence or suicide. Your job is not to comment, fix, or interpret. Receive it. "Thank you for trusting us with that." A long pause is appropriate. Then, gently, move on. The room can hold heavy stories if you do not panic.

Cultural Variation in Funeral Practices

Funeral and burial practices vary widely across cultures and faiths. Some participants may have customs around how a body is handled, how mourning is observed, or how a service is conducted that are different from what the books describe. The books offer a generic framework. Cultural and religious traditions take precedence in any specific family. Make space for participants to name their own traditions when they come up.

NOTES

REPRODUCIBLE HANDOUTS

Module 3

The following pages may be photocopied for classroom use.
Each handout is designed to fit a single 8.5 × 11 page.

HANDOUT 3A

The First 72 Hours at a Glance

REPRODUCIBLE HANDOUT

Use this as a reference if you ever need it, or as a teaching tool to share with your family.

The First 24 Hours

1. Get a legal pronouncement of death (911, hospice, or facility staff).
2. Notify immediate family. Ask one or two people to help with extended notifications.
3. Arrange care for dependents (children, elderly relatives) and pets.
4. Select a funeral home for transport. *You can change funeral homes later if needed.*
5. Secure the home. Lock doors, manage mail, take care of plants and pets.
6. Take care of yourself. Drink water. Eat. Rest. Accept help.

The Next 72 Hours

1. Gather key documents: birth certificate, Social Security card, marriage certificate, military papers, insurance policies, will or trust documents.
2. Notify employer (for pay and benefits), religious or cultural leader, close friends, community.
3. Meet with a funeral director and begin discussing service details.
4. Write or arrange for an obituary if desired.
5. Handle immediate practical matters: cancel medical appointments, notify landlord if applicable, secure vehicles and personal property.
6. Begin family conversations about service plans, who will speak, what music, and so on.
7. Continue caring for yourself and accepting help.

REMEMBER

You do not have to do everything in the first 72 hours.

You do have to take the next step.

Funeral homes are required by federal law to give you a price list. Compare prices. You do not have to buy the most expensive option.

If your loved one prepaid for arrangements, that paperwork is critical. Find it.

HANDOUT 3B

Funeral and Memorial Decisions Worksheet

REPRODUCIBLE HANDOUT

This worksheet has two parts. Part 1 is for you to record your own preferences — the gift you can leave your family. Part 2 is for use if you are ever planning a service for someone else.

Part 1 · My Own Preferences

Burial or cremation:

If burial, location of plot or wishes:

If cremation, what should be done with remains:

Type of service I want:

Religious tradition (or none):

Preferred location:

Officiant I would want, if any:

Music or readings I would want included:

Anyone I would specifically want to speak:

Anything I do not want included:

Donations in lieu of flowers, and to what cause:

Any other wishes:

HANDOUT 3B (CONTINUED)

Funeral and Memorial Decisions — Part 2

REPRODUCIBLE HANDOUT

Part 2 · Planning a Service for Someone Else

Use this list as a checklist if you are ever the person making these decisions.

Burial or cremation? Have prearrangements been made?

Type of service? Where? When?

Officiant? Music? Readings? Speakers?

Casket or urn? Flowers? Programs?

Obituary written and submitted?

Reception or gathering after the service?

Family members and close friends notified of all details?

Notes

HANDOUT 3C

Reading and Reflection for Week 4

REPRODUCIBLE HANDOUT

Reading

If you have *When a Loved One Dies*, read Chapters 4, 5, and 6 (Essential Documents and Accounts, Legal Matters, Digital Life).

If you have *Not My Favorite Subject Either, But...*, read Chapters 7, 8, and 9 (Digital Afterlife, Personal Legacy Projects, Organizing the "Final Binder").

If you have both books, read the primary chapters from *When a Loved One Dies* and the parallel chapters from *Not My Favorite Subject Either, But...*

Reflection Questions

1. Make a list — just a quick mental list — of all the online accounts you have. How long is the list? Who would have access if you could not?

2. If someone had to settle your estate tomorrow, where would the most time be lost? What information would be hardest to find?

App Activity

Read at least one of these three free articles in the Resource hub of the Life Now & Beyond app: "*The First 24 Hours*," "*The Next 72 Hours*," or "*Preparing for Services*." Optional: preview the After-Loss Guidance & Support workspace from the home screen. The workspace itself is a premium feature, but the articles cover the information at no cost.

WEEK FOUR

MODULE

04

Documents, Legal Matters, and Digital Life

The paperwork that follows — and the digital legacy each of us now carries.

Module Overview

Module 4 covers the paperwork-heavy middle weeks after a death and the digital legacy that everyone now carries. This is the most logistical module in the course. Much of the material is technical: probate basics, executor duties, account closures, social media memorialization, password access. The teaching segments need to be clear and concrete without overwhelming participants with details that vary by state.

This module also addresses what is, for many people, the single most overlooked part of preparation: the digital life. Almost everyone has dozens of online accounts. Almost no one has documented how their family would access them. The cost of this oversight has grown sharply in the last decade and will only grow further.

The combined content of this module pulls heavily from both books — Chapters 4 through 6 of When a Loved One Dies for the after-death documentation work, and Chapters 7 through 9 of Not My Favorite Subject Either, But… for the preparation work, including the "final binder" concept that ties everything together.

Learning Objectives

By the end of Module 4, participants will be able to:

- Identify the key documents needed in the weeks after a death, including death certificates and account-related paperwork
- Describe the role of an executor and the basics of when probate is required
- Recognize the major categories of digital accounts that need to be managed after a death
- Explain the concept of a "final binder" and what it should contain
- Identify their own next step in organizing their personal documents and digital life

Materials Needed

- Teacher's Guide
- Sign-in sheet, tissues, water
- Reproducible Handout 4A: Documents Needed After a Death
- Reproducible Handout 4B: My Final Binder Table of Contents
- Reproducible Handout 4C: Reading and Reflection for Week 5

Lesson Plan with Timing

Recommended session length: 60 minutes. Plan for 60 to 90 minutes to allow for natural discussion. *Module 4 sometimes runs slightly shorter than other modules because the content is more technical and discussion is more focused.*

TIME	SEGMENT	PURPOSE
0:00 – 0:05	**Welcome and Reconnection**	Brief check-in.
0:05 – 0:20	**Documents and Legal Matters After a Death**	Death certificates, executor role, probate basics.
0:20 – 0:35	**Digital Life and Digital Legacy**	Categories of accounts, password access, social media, digital files.
0:35 – 0:50	**Activity: Build Your Final Binder Table of Contents**	Participants complete Handout 4B. Share in pairs. *Flex point.*
0:50 – 0:57	**Discussion**	What did you discover? What surprised you?
0:57 – 1:00	**Closing and Preview of Module 5**	Distribute reading. Close warmly.

Teacher's Script and Talking Points

Welcome and Reconnection (5 minutes)

> *"Welcome back. Last week we walked through the first 72 hours and the planning of services. Tonight we cover the middle weeks — the paperwork that follows, and the digital life that has to be managed. This is the most logistical session of the course. There is a lot of detail. The goal is not to memorize anything tonight. The goal is to know what categories of work exist and to have a sense of where you want to start in organizing your own life.*

Documents and Legal Matters After a Death (15 minutes)

Here is the truth about the weeks after a death. **While the family is grieving, someone has to handle a small mountain of paperwork.** The work falls heaviest on the executor of the estate, but the family supports them.

The first essential document is the **death certificate**. You will need certified copies, not photocopies. Order more than you think you need — typically 10 to 15 — because almost every institution that needs to be notified will ask for one and many will not return it. Banks, life insurance companies, the Social Security Administration, retirement account custodians, the IRS, and so on. Each one wants its own copy. The funeral home usually orders these for you. Make sure they order enough.

The next category is **personal identity documents**: the deceased's Social Security card, birth certificate, marriage certificate, military discharge papers, and any other identity documents. These need to be located and kept secure. Some are needed for benefits, some for proof of relationships, some for closing accounts.

Then there are **financial and insurance documents**: bank statements, investment accounts, retirement accounts, life insurance policies, mortgage documents, vehicle titles, and anything else that proves what the deceased owned and owed. You will need to find all of these before the executor can do their work.

Then **legal documents**: the will, any trust documents, any powers of attorney, business papers if applicable, and any pre-arranged funeral or burial documents.

Now, about the **executor**. The executor is the person named in the will to handle the estate. If there is no will, a court appoints someone, usually a close family member. The executor's job is to gather all the assets, pay all the debts and taxes, and distribute what is left according to the will or state law. It is a significant amount of work. It can take months and sometimes years for complicated estates.

Probate is the court process by which a will is validated and the executor is officially authorized to act. Probate is required in most cases, with major exceptions: assets held in a properly funded trust avoid probate. Assets held jointly with right of survivorship pass automatically to the other owner. Accounts with named beneficiaries — like life insurance policies, retirement accounts, and "transfer on death" accounts — pass directly to the beneficiary without probate.

Probate laws vary by state. Some states have streamlined small-estate procedures. Some have lengthy and expensive probate processes. This is one of the major reasons people set up trusts — to avoid probate. Whether you need to worry about this depends entirely on your state and your assets. *An estate planning attorney is the right person to ask.*

A NOTE ON DEBTS

When someone dies, their debts do not automatically transfer to family members. The estate pays the debts, and if there is not enough money in the estate, many debts simply go unpaid. There are exceptions — jointly held debts, certain types of medical debt in certain states, debts secured by property like mortgages. But in general, family members are not personally responsible for the deceased's credit card debt. *If a debt collector contacts you and tries to make you feel personally responsible, that is a tactic, not the law.* Get advice from an attorney before paying any debt of a deceased person out of your own money.

Digital Life and Digital Legacy (15 minutes)

Now we turn to digital life. This is the area that most people, even prepared people, have not really addressed. And it is the area that has grown the fastest.

Think for a moment about all the online accounts you have. Email — probably more than one. Banking and finance. Investment accounts. Social media — Facebook, Instagram, LinkedIn, TikTok, X, possibly more. Cloud storage where your photos and documents live. Subscription services for streaming, news, software. Shopping accounts. Cryptocurrency wallets, possibly. Business accounts. Loyalty programs. Healthcare portals. Maybe a website or domain you own.

> "*Now ask: who else can access any of those if you cannot? Probably no one, or almost no one. That is the digital legacy problem.*

When someone dies, the digital accounts are still there. Email keeps receiving messages. Subscriptions keep auto-renewing. Photos sit in cloud accounts that no one can get into. Memorial pages get spammed by hackers. Some accounts go into limbo for years.

Here is the basic structure of how to handle this:

1. **Create an inventory.** Every account, what type, what email it is associated with. The account itself, not the password.
2. **Manage the passwords separately.** The standard recommendation is a password manager — a piece of software that holds all your passwords behind one master password. The advantage is that you only need to communicate one piece of information to your trusted person: how to access the password manager. They can then access everything else.
3. **Handle social media intentionally.** Most major platforms now have memorialization or legacy features. Facebook lets you appoint a "legacy contact" who can manage your account after your death. Apple has a Digital Legacy program. Google has an Inactive Account Manager. *Set these up while you are alive.*
4. **Handle subscription services.** After a death, recurring charges keep happening until someone cancels them. Months can go by before a family realizes they are still paying for services no one is using. Document where the recurring charges are.

5. **Preserve digital memories.** Photos, videos, written documents — the things future generations will want. These need to be in a place where someone other than the deceased can find them. A *locked cloud account that nobody can access is not preservation.*

6. **Special handling for cryptocurrency and complex digital assets.** If you own cryptocurrency and the access keys die with you, your family loses the assets entirely. There is no customer service department to call. This is increasingly common and increasingly tragic. If you have any meaningful crypto holdings, you must address access in your estate planning.

The Final Binder Concept

All of this — the documents, the legal information, the digital inventory — needs to live somewhere that someone other than you can find. The simple solution is what Alice Truman calls the **"final binder."** It is a single physical or digital location that contains everything. A binder, a folder in a fireproof box, a secure cloud location, or some combination.

What goes in it: a personal letter to your family explaining where everything is. The legal documents. The financial inventory. The healthcare directives. The funeral preferences. The digital inventory. A list of important contacts — attorney, accountant, financial advisor, insurance agent, doctor. And, often, a personal letter or video message that has nothing to do with logistics, just love.

The Life Now & Beyond app implements this concept directly. Its Life Binder is organized into the same categories we have been working through: Personal Information, Medical Information, Insurance Policies, Financial Information, Legal Documents, Final Wishes, and Digital Legacy. Three of those sections are free, four are premium. And the app's Trusted Access feature solves the access problem we just talked about — it lets you designate trusted people who can reach the information when they need to.

THIS IS THE CONVERSION MOMENT FOR THE APP

The free tier of the app gives you up to three trusted contacts, and you can configure each one with a specific permission level: Medical Information Only, Legal Documents Only, Financial Overview Only, or Full Emergency Access. That is real protection. **But the trusted people you designate can only see the Life Binder sections you have actually populated** — which on the free tier is three of seven.

Premium ($49/year) completes the protection. It unlocks the four remaining Life Binder sections, removes the limit on trusted contacts, and adds document uploads. *The choice of whether to upgrade is yours.* Some participants may decide premium is worth it; others will continue with paper-based work for the four premium sections. Both are valid. The course works either way.

Activity: Build Your Final Binder Table of Contents (15 minutes)

Distribute Handout 4B. Give participants 8 minutes to fill it out, then 5 minutes to share in pairs. Reserve the last 2 minutes for a brief group debrief before the discussion segment.

> *Here is the activity. On the handout I just gave you, build the table of contents for your own final binder. Just the table of contents — do not try to fill in the actual information. Eight minutes. Then turn to a neighbor and compare lists for five minutes. You will be surprised at what shows up on someone else's list that did not show up on yours.*

Discussion (7 minutes)

- What was on someone else's list that you had not thought of?
- What is the single hardest item on your list to actually pull together?
- Who in your life would you give access to this binder, and how would you communicate that?

Closing and Preview of Module 5 (3 minutes)

> *Next week we shift away from logistics and into the heart of the course: grief, family dynamics, and self-care. We will talk about how grief actually shows up, how families respond to loss, how to take care of yourself, and how to begin the conversations with the people you love that this course has been preparing you for. Thank you for tonight. I will see you next week.*

Reading Assignments for Next Week

If your participants have *When a Loved One Dies*: Primary reading: Chapters 7, 8, 9, 10, and 11 (Grief and the Family Circle, Caring for Yourself in the Midst of Loss, Special Circumstances, Modern Family Dynamics, Crisis Scenarios).

If your participants have *Not My Favorite Subject Either, But...*: Primary reading: Chapters 10 and 11 (Talking With Loved Ones, Spiritual and Emotional Closure).

If your participants have both books: Read the primary chapters from both. Together they cover both how grief unfolds after a loss and how to have the conversations now that prevent some of that grief from being unnecessarily complicated.

App Integration

Module 4 is the natural moment in the course where premium features become directly useful. The Digital Legacy section of the Life Binder is premium-only. The Trusted Access feature, which participants have been able to configure with three contacts on the free tier, becomes a deeper conversation here.

THIS WEEK, IN THE APP

In the Life Now & Beyond app, take a careful look at the Digital Legacy section of the Life Binder. It is premium-only, but you can preview it. Take a few minutes to look at your current Trusted Access configuration: who do you have, what permission level have you given them, and what would they actually see today if they triggered emergency access? **That is the real test.** If you decide premium is worth it, this is the natural week. If not, keep building your table of contents on paper.

Sensitivity Notes

Technical Overwhelm

This is the most technical module in the course. Some participants will feel out of their depth on legal and financial topics. Reassure them: nobody is expected to become an expert tonight. The course is helping them know what questions to ask and where to ask them.

Digital Confidence Varies Widely

In any group, you will have participants who are highly comfortable with technology and participants who are not. The "build your digital inventory" framing can feel daunting to less tech-confident participants. Emphasize that any inventory is better than no inventory, and that pen-and-paper is a valid tool.

Cryptocurrency, Business Ownership, and Other Specialized Topics

A small number of participants will have specialized assets that need specialized planning. The course can flag these issues; it cannot solve them. Refer participants with significant cryptocurrency holdings, business ownership, intellectual property, or international assets to a specialized estate planning attorney.

Family Members Stuck in Estate Limbo

Some participants are currently stuck in long, painful estate processes for relatives who died years ago. The teaching content can rekindle frustration. Acknowledge this when it surfaces and direct participants toward attorneys who specialize in estate disputes if they need help moving forward.

NOTES

REPRODUCIBLE HANDOUTS

Module 4

The following pages may be photocopied for classroom use.
Each handout is designed to fit a single 8.5 × 11 page.

HANDOUT 4A

Documents Needed After a Death

REPRODUCIBLE HANDOUT

A reference list of the major categories of documents that surface in the weeks after a death.

Death Certificate

Order 10 to 15 certified copies. The funeral home usually handles the order. Each institution that needs notification will require its own copy.

Personal Identity Documents

- Social Security card
- Birth certificate
- Marriage certificate (if applicable)
- Divorce decree (if applicable)
- Military discharge papers (DD-214 for veterans)
- Naturalization or immigration papers (if applicable)

Financial and Insurance Documents

- Bank statements and account information
- Investment and retirement account statements
- Life insurance policies
- Mortgage documents and other loan paperwork
- Vehicle titles
- Property deeds
- Recent tax returns

Legal Documents

- Will
- Trust documents
- Powers of attorney (financial and healthcare)
- Advance healthcare directive
- Pre-arranged funeral or burial documents
- Business ownership papers (if applicable)

Digital Access Information

- Password manager access
- List of online accounts
- Social media legacy contact information
- Cloud storage access

- Cryptocurrency wallet access (if applicable)

HANDOUT 4B

My Final Binder Table of Contents

REPRODUCIBLE HANDOUT

Build the table of contents for your own final binder. Do not try to fill in the actual information yet. Just list what should be in the binder. Use the categories below as starting points and add anything specific to your situation.

NOTE

The Life Now & Beyond app's Life Binder is organized around these same seven categories: Personal Information, Medical Information, Insurance Policies, Financial Information, Legal Documents, Final Wishes, and Digital Legacy. Three sections are free; four require premium ($49/year). Your work here translates directly into the app whenever you are ready.

Section 1 · A Letter to My Family — A personal letter explaining where to find everything and what you want them to know.

HANDOUT 4B (CONTINUED)

Sections 2 through 9

Section 2 · Legal Documents

Section 3 · Financial Information

Section 4 · Healthcare and End-of-Life Wishes

Section 5 · Funeral and Memorial Preferences

Section 6 · Digital Life

Section 7 · Important Contacts

Section 8 · Personal Messages and Legacy

Section 9 · Other (Specific to Me)

HANDOUT 4C

Reading and Reflection for Week 5

REPRODUCIBLE HANDOUT

Reading

If you have *When a Loved One Dies*, read Chapters 7 through 11 (Grief and the Family Circle, Caring for Yourself in the Midst of Loss, Special Circumstances, Modern Family Dynamics, Crisis Scenarios).

If you have *Not My Favorite Subject Either, But…*, read Chapters 10 and 11 (Talking With Loved Ones, Spiritual and Emotional Closure).

If you have both books, read the primary chapters from both.

Reflection Questions

1. Think of a loss you have experienced — yours or someone else's. What was one thing that helped during the grief? What was one thing that did not help, even when it was meant to?

2. Who in your life is hardest to talk to about death and grief? Why?

App Activity

In the Life Now & Beyond app, look at the Digital Legacy section of the Life Binder (premium-only — you can preview it). Review your current Trusted Access setup: who is on it, what permissions you assigned, and what they would actually see today. If premium feels worth $49 a year for the protection it gives your family, this is the natural week to upgrade. If not, keep building your table of contents on paper.

WEEK FIVE

MODULE

05

Grief, Family, and Self-Care

The emotional center of the course.

Module Overview

Module 5 is the emotional center of the course. After four sessions on framing, preparation, aftermath, and logistics, this module turns to the human heart of the experience: how grief actually shows up in our lives, how families respond to loss, how to care for ourselves in the middle of it, and how to begin the conversations with our loved ones that this course has been preparing us for.

This is the module that participants will most often describe later as the one that meant the most to them. It is also the module most likely to evoke deep emotion. Pace yourself. Pace the room. The teaching content is real, but the heart of the session is the discussion and the activity.

Learning Objectives

By the end of Module 5, participants will be able to:

- Describe how grief commonly shows up, including its non-linear nature and the wide variety of valid grieving styles
- Recognize how grief can change family dynamics and create unexpected conflict
- Identify several concrete self-care practices appropriate for someone in grief
- Articulate why having end-of-life conversations with loved ones in advance is one of the most generous things they can do
- Identify one specific conversation they want to have with a specific person in the coming weeks

Materials Needed

- Teacher's Guide
- Sign-in sheet, tissues, water
- Reproducible Handout 5A: How Grief Actually Shows Up
- Reproducible Handout 5B: A Conversation I Need to Have
- Reproducible Handout 5C: Reading and Reflection for Week 6

Lesson Plan with Timing

Recommended session length: 60 minutes. Plan for 60 to 90 minutes. *This module almost always runs long. Reserve the room for the full 90 minutes.*

TIME	SEGMENT	PURPOSE
0:00 – 0:05	**Welcome and Reconnection**	Brief check-in. Note that tonight is the emotional heart of the course.
0:05 – 0:20	**Teaching: How Grief Actually Shows Up**	Common patterns, individual variation, family dynamics.
0:20 – 0:30	**Teaching: Self-Care in Grief**	Practical strategies for taking care of yourself.
0:30 – 0:42	**Teaching: The Conversations We Need to Have**	How to begin end-of-life conversations with loved ones.
0:42 – 0:52	**Activity: A Conversation I Need to Have**	Participants complete Handout 5B. Pair sharing. *Flex point.*
0:52 – 0:57	**Discussion**	Open discussion drawing on the teaching and activity.
0:57 – 1:00	**Closing and Preview of Module 6**	Distribute reading. Close warmly.

Teacher's Script and Talking Points

Welcome and Reconnection (5 minutes)

> “ *Welcome back. Tonight is the emotional heart of the course. We are going to talk about grief, about families, about caring for ourselves, and about the conversations we owe the people we love. Some of what we cover tonight may be hard. Take your time. Pass when you need to. And know that we are nearing the end of this work together — next week is our final session.*

How Grief Actually Shows Up (15 minutes)

Most of us grew up with a vague idea that grief has stages — denial, anger, bargaining, depression, acceptance. That model came from research on people facing their own deaths, not on people grieving losses. It has been widely misapplied. **Grief is not a staircase. It is not a checklist. You do not graduate from one stage to the next.**

What grief actually looks like is more like waves. Sometimes you are okay for hours, even days. Then a song plays, or a smell hits you, or a date arrives, and the grief returns. Sometimes the wave is small. Sometimes it knocks you down. Over time, the waves usually come less often and feel less violent, but they do not necessarily stop.

Grief also shows up differently in different people. Some people cry constantly. Others go numb. Some people want to talk about the person they lost, often. Others cannot bear to say the name. Some people want to keep busy. Others can barely get out of bed. Some people feel a strange relief, especially after a long illness, and then guilt for feeling that relief.

> *All of this is normal. There is no right way to grieve. There is only the way you are doing it.*

Now, here is where it gets complicated. Different family members grieve differently. After a death, you have a family of people who all loved the same person, all in some kind of pain, and all expressing it differently. The husband who never cries is not avoiding his grief; he is grieving in his way. The daughter who organizes everything is not being cold; she is grieving in her way. The son who disappears for days is not abandoning the family; he is grieving in his way.

When family members do not understand each other's grieving styles, it can become a source of real conflict. People accuse each other of not caring enough, of caring too much, of not crying, of crying too much. Old family wounds reopen. Decisions about the funeral, the estate, the belongings, become fights about something deeper.

THREE THINGS TO KNOW ABOUT GRIEF

There is no comparison. The way you grieve is the right way for you. The way they grieve is the right way for them. Try not to police each other.

Grief is not a problem to solve. It is a process to live through. The goal is not to get over it. The goal is to integrate the loss into a life that continues. There is no timeline.

Sometimes grief needs professional help. If grief is preventing someone from functioning months or years after a loss, if they are talking about wanting to die, if they are unable to find any moments of peace, that is a signal to seek a grief counselor or therapist. Grief counseling is not a sign of failure. It is a sign of taking the loss seriously enough to want help with it.

Self-Care in Grief (10 minutes)

Now let us talk about self-care, because grieving people are often terrible at it. The body and mind are doing extraordinary work in grief, and they need support. Here are some concrete practices that help.

1. **Basic physical needs.** Drink water. Eat regularly, even when you do not feel like it. Sleep when you can, even if it is fragmented. Move your body, even just a walk around the block. Grief takes a physical toll. The body needs help.

2. **Small rituals.** Small daily anchors help: a cup of tea at the same time each morning, a short walk, a moment of quiet, lighting a candle in memory. These are not silly. They are how the body and the mind regulate themselves through hard times.

3. **Boundaries with other people.** Grieving people are often expected to perform recovery for the comfort of others. You do not have to. You are allowed to decline social events. You are allowed to leave gatherings early. You are allowed to say, "I am not ready to talk about this."

4. **Accepting help without guilt.** People often want to help and do not know how. Let them. Let someone bring you food. Let someone sit with you. Let someone walk your dog. Accepting help is not weakness; it is one of the most loving things you can do for the people who care about you.

5. **Professional support when needed.** Grief counselors, therapists, support groups, hospice bereavement programs — these resources exist for a reason. You do not have to do this alone, and using these resources does not mean you are doing grief wrong.

6. **Watching for signs that grief is becoming something more.** Persistent thoughts of self-harm, complete inability to function for an extended period, severe substance use that is escalating, complete withdrawal from everyone you love. *If any of these are happening, please reach out for help.*

The Conversations We Need to Have (12 minutes)

Now I want to turn to the other half of this module: the conversations. We have spent five sessions preparing for what happens when we lose someone we love and what happens when we die ourselves. **None of that preparation matters very much if we never actually talk to the people we love about it.**

Most adults have never had a substantive conversation with their parents about their parents' wishes. Most parents have never had a substantive conversation with their adult children about what they want when they die. Most spouses know less than they think they do about each other's wishes. We assume we will get to it eventually. Eventually arrives, usually, only after it is too late.

> *Here is the thing about these conversations. They are not as hard as we think. The hardest part is starting them.*

A few practical thoughts on how to begin.

1. **Pick the right moment.** Not at a holiday dinner with everyone watching. Not when one of you is upset about something else. A quiet evening at home, a long drive, a walk — these are the settings where these conversations actually happen.

2. **Give yourself an opening.** You can use this course as one. "*I have been taking a class about end-of-life planning, and it has me thinking about us. Can we talk about it?*" That is a complete opening. Most people will say yes.

3. **Share your own thinking first.** "*I have started writing down what I would want for a funeral. I want you to know what I am thinking. I would also love to know what you would want, when you are ready to talk about it.*" Leading with your own work makes the conversation reciprocal and lowers the pressure on the other person.
4. **Accept incremental progress.** The conversation does not have to cover everything in one sitting. You may have one conversation, then another a few weeks later, then another a few months after that. Each one moves you forward. Each one is a gift.
5. **Write things down.** Conversations are wonderful but memory is unreliable. After a meaningful conversation about end-of-life wishes, write down what was said. Share what you wrote with the person to confirm. This way the conversation actually translates into something usable later.
6. **Accept that some people will not engage.** A spouse, a parent, a sibling may flatly refuse to discuss any of this. You cannot force them. What you can do is have your own affairs in order, document what you do know about their wishes, and leave the door open. Sometimes the conversation happens later, when something else changes.

Activity: A Conversation I Need to Have (10 minutes)

Distribute Handout 5B. Give participants 5 minutes to fill it out, then 5 minutes to share in pairs.

> "*On the handout I just gave you, identify one specific conversation you need to have with one specific person, and start to plan it. Take 5 minutes. Then turn to a neighbor and share what you wrote, for another 5 minutes. The point of sharing it out loud is that saying it makes it more real. People who name the conversation out loud are significantly more likely to actually have it.*

Discussion (5 minutes)

- What did you notice while doing the activity? What came up?
- Has anyone in this group already had one of these conversations? What worked?
- What would help you actually have the conversation you wrote down?

Closing and Preview of Module 6 (3 minutes)

> "*Next week is our final session. We will look at what comes after the immediate grief: the long journey through anniversaries, holidays, secondary losses, and the slow rebuilding of a life. We will also talk about legacy — not legacy in some grand sense, but the legacy each of us is leaving every day, and what we want to make of the rest of our lives.*

A SMALL ASSIGNMENT FOR THIS WEEK

Between now and next week, try to begin the conversation you wrote down on tonight's handout. Even five minutes. Even just opening the door. **Just begin it.** Thank you for tonight, and I will see you next week for our last session.

Reading Assignments for Next Week

If your participants have *When a Loved One Dies*: Primary reading: Chapters 12 and 13 (Life After the Funeral, Preparing for the Future).

If your participants have *Not My Favorite Subject Either, But...*: Primary reading: Chapter 12 (Living Well Until the End).

If your participants have both books: Read all three chapters. Together they tell a complete story: how to live forward after a loss, and how to live fully knowing the end is coming.

App Integration

The app's Conversation Starters feature is built for exactly the work tonight's activity asks participants to do: difficult but necessary conversations about wishes, care preferences, aging decisions, family roles, and legacy. The free tier offers a starter set of prompts that should cover what most participants need for tonight's exercise. Premium expands this to a full library.

THIS WEEK, IN THE APP

Look through the Conversation Starters. Pick one that fits the conversation you wrote down on Handout 5B and use it to begin. The starter set on the free tier should give you a prompt that fits. The Planning Journal is also there if you want a private place to record what comes up.

Sensitivity Notes

This Module Will Make People Cry

More than any other session, Module 5 will produce tears. That is appropriate to the material. Have tissues visible. Allow for pauses. If multiple participants are emotional at once, slow down. The room can hold it.

Estranged Relationships

Some participants are estranged from family members and the conversation about "having the conversation" can be painful. Make space for the reality that not every conversation can be had, and not every person can be reached. The goal is not to fix every relationship. The goal is to do what is possible from where you stand.

Recent Bereavement

Participants in fresh grief may find this module either deeply healing or deeply hard, sometimes both within minutes. Check in with anyone you know is in fresh grief. Offer the option of stepping out, especially during the teaching segment on grief itself.

Watch for Signs of Complicated Grief

This module is when complicated grief most often becomes visible to a teacher. If during discussion you hear a participant describing prolonged inability to function, persistent thoughts of dying themselves, or complete inability to find any moments of peace, plan to speak with that person privately after the session and offer professional referral resources. Use the language: "What you are describing sounds really heavy. Have you thought about talking to a grief counselor? They can help."

NOTES

REPRODUCIBLE HANDOUTS

Module 5

The following pages may be photocopied for classroom use. Each handout is designed to fit a single 8.5 × 11 page.

HANDOUT 5A

How Grief Actually Shows Up

REPRODUCIBLE HANDOUT

A reference for understanding your own grief and the grief of people around you.

Grief Is Not Linear

Grief moves in waves, not stages. You can be okay for hours and then knocked down by a song or a smell. Over time, the waves come less often, but they may not stop entirely.

Grief Looks Different in Different People

- Some cry constantly. Some go numb. Both are valid.
- Some want to talk about the person. Some cannot bear to say the name.
- Some want to stay busy. Some can barely get out of bed.
- Some feel relief, especially after long illness, and then guilt about feeling relief.
- Some grieve loudly. Some grieve privately.

Grief in Families

Family members grieving the same loss in different ways often misread each other. The husband who does not cry is not uncaring. The daughter who organizes is not unfeeling. The son who withdraws is not abandoning anyone. *Each is grieving in their way.*

Self-Care Practices That Help

- Drink water. Eat regularly. Sleep when you can. Move your body, even gently.
- Build small daily rituals: a cup of tea, a walk, a candle, a moment of quiet.
- Set boundaries. You can decline events, leave early, and ask for space.
- Accept help. Let people bring food, sit with you, run errands.
- Consider professional support. Grief counselors, therapists, support groups, hospice bereavement programs.

When to Seek Professional Help

- Persistent inability to function in daily life weeks or months after the loss
- Thoughts of self-harm or wanting to die
- Severe substance use that has emerged or worsened
- Complete withdrawal from everyone
- Inability to find any moments of peace, ever

IF YOU ARE IN CRISIS

Call or text **988** (Suicide and Crisis Lifeline).
Contact your primary care doctor or a mental health professional.
Reach out to someone you trust and tell them what is happening.
You do not have to do this alone.

HANDOUT 5B

A Conversation I Need to Have

REPRODUCIBLE HANDOUT

Identify one specific conversation you need to have with one specific person. Use this handout to plan it.

Who is the person?

What is the conversation about?

What has stopped me from having this conversation so far?

When and where could I begin this conversation? (Be specific. A particular evening, a particular setting.)

What is one sentence I could use to open the conversation?

What outcome would I be happy with from a first conversation? (Remember: you do not have to cover everything in one sitting.)

What is the single first step I will take this week?

HANDOUT 5C

Reading and Reflection for Week 6

REPRODUCIBLE HANDOUT

Reading

If you have *When a Loved One Dies*, read Chapters 12 and 13 (Life After the Funeral, Preparing for the Future).

If you have *Not My Favorite Subject Either, But...*, read Chapter 12 (Living Well Until the End).

If you have both books, read all three chapters.

Reflection Questions

1. Looking back over the past five weeks, what has shifted in you? What do you understand differently than you did at the start?

2. What would you most want to remember from this course six months from now? Twelve months from now?

App Activity

In the Life Now & Beyond app, open Conversation Starters from the home screen. Read through the starter set of prompts (free) and pick one to use for the conversation you identified on Handout 5B. If you have premium, the full library includes specialized prompts for blended families, estranged relationships, business succession, and other specific situations.

> **A REMINDER**
>
> Try to begin the conversation you identified on Handout 5B this week. **Even five minutes. Even just opening the door.**

WEEK SIX

MODULE

06

Moving Forward and Leaving a Legacy

The closing of the course — and the beginning of a new way of living.

Module Overview

Module 6 closes the course. Tonight we cover what happens after the immediate aftermath of grief — the long, slow rebuilding of a life that includes the loss. Anniversaries, holidays, secondary losses, finding meaning. We also turn the camera around: what is the legacy each of us is leaving every day, and what do we want to do with the time we have?

This module is about closing well. It is about looking back at what the group has done together and looking forward at what each participant will carry into the rest of their lives. Many participants will arrive at the final session with a mix of emotions — sad that the course is ending, proud of what they have done, sometimes anxious about losing the structure and the community that the course has provided.

Your job tonight is to help them mark the ending well, give them a clear sense of what they will carry forward, and send them out with both hands full.

Learning Objectives

By the end of Module 6, participants will be able to:

- Describe the longer arc of grief beyond the first weeks and months, including anniversaries, holidays, and secondary losses
- Identify ways to honor and remember a loved one over time
- Articulate what living well in light of mortality means to them personally
- Name a specific legacy they want to leave — in their family, in their community, in their work, or in their character
- Commit to specific next steps for continuing the work this course has started

Materials Needed

- Teacher's Guide
- Sign-in sheet, tissues, water
- Reproducible Handout 6A: Living Forward After a Loss
- Reproducible Handout 6B: My Six-Month Plan
- Reproducible Handout 6C: A Letter to My Future Self
- Resource list of grief support, legal, financial, and other community resources (you provide based on your local area)

Lesson Plan with Timing

Recommended session length: 60 minutes. Plan for 60 to 90 minutes. *The final session deserves space; do not rush it.*

TIME	SEGMENT	PURPOSE
0:00 – 0:05	**Welcome and Recognition**	Acknowledge that this is the final session. Briefly look back at what the group has done together.
0:05 – 0:18	**Teaching: Living Forward After a Loss**	Anniversaries, holidays, secondary losses, rebuilding.
0:18 – 0:30	**Teaching: Living Well and Leaving a Legacy**	What it means to live with mortality in view, and what we leave behind.
0:30 – 0:42	**Activity: My Six-Month Plan**	Participants commit to specific next steps. Pair sharing.
0:42 – 0:52	**A Letter to My Future Self**	Quiet writing exercise. Sealed and self-addressed.
0:52 – 0:58	**Closing Discussion**	What are you taking with you?
0:58 – 1:00	**Final Words and Goodbye**	A short closing.

Teacher's Script and Talking Points

Welcome and Recognition (5 minutes)

> *"Welcome to our final session. I want to begin tonight by acknowledging what we have done together. Six weeks ago, you walked into this room knowing this was a course about death and grief. Most people would not have come. You did. Over six sessions, you have worked through the conversation we avoid, the practical preparation, the immediate aftermath, the documents and digital life, the heart of grief and family, and now — tonight — the question of how to live forward.*

I am proud of you. I want you to feel proud of yourselves. Tonight is about closing well. We are going to look at what comes after the immediate grief, what it means to live well with mortality in view, what kind of legacy each of you wants to leave, and what specifically you are going to carry forward from this work.

Living Forward After a Loss (13 minutes)

Most of what is written about grief focuses on the first weeks and months. Less is said about the longer arc — the months and years that come after the casseroles stop arriving, after the cards fade, after the rest of the world has moved on. **That long arc is where most grieving actually lives.**

There are some predictable patterns in this longer journey. Knowing them helps.

1. **Anniversaries hit hard.** The first anniversary of the death is often the most intense. But birthdays, wedding anniversaries, and other meaningful dates can also bring sharp returns of grief, sometimes for years. Holidays — especially Thanksgiving, Christmas, and any holiday the deceased loved — can be especially difficult. The first time around the calendar without your person is its own grieving process.
2. **Secondary losses arrive.** After the immediate loss of the person, you discover other losses you did not anticipate. The loss of the future you had imagined. The loss of identity — if you were a wife and now you are a widow, who are you? The loss of the friend group you shared with the deceased. The loss of the role you played in the family.
3. **Daily routines have to be rebuilt.** Mealtimes, sleep, work patterns, social rhythms — all of it needs new shape. This rebuilding takes time. Be patient with yourself. New routines emerge slowly.
4. **You find ways to honor and remember.** Many people develop personal rituals — a charity in the name of the deceased, an annual visit to a meaningful place, a candle lit on the anniversary, a recipe made every year. These rituals are not about being stuck in the loss. They are about integrating the loss into a continuing life.
5. **Social connections rebuild gradually.** Some friendships will not survive. Some friends did not know how to be present. Other friends will surprise you with their faithfulness. New friendships will form. The social world after a major loss is different from the one before.
6. **Life direction reopens.** Many people who have been through significant grief eventually find that their priorities have changed. Things that mattered before do not matter as much. Things they were postponing rise to the surface. *This is not a phase to rush through. It is one of the gifts grief sometimes leaves — a clearer sense of what matters.*

Living Well and Leaving a Legacy (12 minutes)

The other half of this final module is about how we live, knowing what we know now. The whole arc of this course is built around the recognition that we are all going to die and that we love people who are also going to die. **What does that recognition mean for how we live?**

A few thoughts.

1. **Mortality is a clarifying force.** When we hold our own death in view — not morbidly, just honestly — the trivial things in our lives shrink. The important things become more visible. People who have had near-death experiences or major illnesses often describe a sharpening of priorities. We do not have to wait for a near-death experience to access this.

2. **Legacy is being created daily.** Most of us think of legacy as something for after we die — the will, the inheritance, the obituary. But legacy is what we leave every day, in every interaction. The way we treat the people in our lives. The kind of parent, spouse, friend, neighbor we are. The work we do. The character we display. *Most of what we will be remembered for is being created in the small, ordinary moments of our lives, right now.*

3. **There is value in writing some of it down.** Many people find it meaningful to leave letters, recordings, or written reflections for the people they love. Letters to children, to be opened later. Recorded stories. Written values, thoughts, memories. None of this is mandatory. All of it can be a gift.

4. **Living fully in the time we have is itself a kind of preparation.** The people who die well are usually the people who lived well. Not lived perfectly, but lived honestly, lovingly, with their priorities in order. The work of this course — having the conversations, organizing the affairs, facing mortality — frees you to live more fully in the time you have.

5. **The work of this course does not end tonight.** You will continue working on your final binder, your conversations, your healthcare directives, your funeral preferences. You will return to the books and the app. You will refine your plans as your life changes. *This is not the end of the work. It is the beginning of a new way of living.*

Activity: My Six-Month Plan (12 minutes)

Distribute Handout 6B. Give participants 7 minutes to fill it out, then 5 minutes for pair sharing.

> *On the handout I just gave you, build a specific six-month plan. Three commitments — just three — that you will make to yourself for what you will accomplish in the next six months. They should be specific. They should be realistic. They should be in writing. Take 7 minutes to write. Then turn to a neighbor and share for 5 minutes. People who say their commitments out loud are significantly more likely to keep them.*

A Letter to My Future Self (10 minutes)

Distribute Handout 6C. Give participants 8 minutes for quiet writing. Provide envelopes if you can; if not, ask participants to fold and seal the letter in some way and write a date six months out on the front.

> *Now I want to give you the most personal exercise of the course. On this handout, write a letter to yourself, to be opened in six months. Write whatever you want your future self to know. What you want to remember from this course. What you want to have done by then. What you want to feel proud of. What you want to forgive yourself for if life has gotten in the way.*

Eight minutes. Quiet writing. When you are done, fold it, seal it if you can, and write a date six months from today on the front. You take the letter home with you. Put it somewhere you will find it. *In six months, open it and read what you wrote tonight.*

Closing Discussion (6 minutes)

Open with a single question.

> *Before we close, I want to ask one question, and I want everyone who feels willing to answer it briefly. What is one thing you are taking with you from this course?*

Go around the room. Some participants will speak briefly; some at length. Honor each. Do not try to summarize or comment after each one.

Final Words and Goodbye (2 minutes)

> *Six weeks ago we began with a simple observation: that we are all going to die, and we love people who are going to die, and that almost no one is prepared for either. Tonight we end with the recognition that you are now more prepared than most. Not finished. Not done. But farther along than you were when you walked in here six weeks ago, and equipped to keep going.*

I want to thank each of you for showing up week after week to face material that most people will not face. I want to thank you for what you brought to this group — your stories, your honesty, your patience with each other. And I want to remind you of one final thing: **the most important work of this course is not what we did in this room. It is what you do from here.**

> *Take care of yourselves. Take care of the people you love. And keep going. Thank you. We are done.*

Reading and Continued Practice

There is no reading assignment after Module 6 — the course is complete. *But the work continues.*

- Encourage participants to revisit chapters of both books that resonated with them.
- Encourage continued use of the LifeNowAndBeyond.com app, particularly for updating documents and tracking progress on six-month commitments.
- Suggest that participants schedule a personal review of their final binder annually — most people pick a meaningful date like a birthday or a New Year.

App Integration

The app supports the work of this final module in several ways. The Planning Journal (free for basic text journaling, premium for rich text and photos) is the natural place to keep the Letter to Future Self and to track progress on the six-month commitments. The Remembrance feature, which is premium for creation but free to view, lets users and families create memorial pages with photos, stories, tributes, and legacy reflections — a meaningful way to honor a loved one over time. After the course, the app becomes the primary tool for ongoing work. The Life Binder is the long-term home of everything participants have started organizing during these six weeks.

THIS WEEK, IN THE APP

Make sure every participant knows that their work in the app continues to be theirs and that they have lifetime reasons to return to it. Update the Life Binder annually. Maintain Trusted Access as the family situation changes. Use Conversation Starters as new conversations arise.

Sensitivity Notes

The Goodbye Itself

Participants will have grown attached to the group over six weeks. Some will be sad about the ending. Some may even cry during the closing. Honor this. The grief of small endings is real and a fitting note for a course about loss. Do not minimize it.

The Letter to Future Self

This activity often produces unexpected emotion. Participants may end up writing things they did not know they were going to write. Allow the room to be quiet during the writing. Resist the urge to talk through it.

What Comes Next for Participants Who Need Ongoing Support

A small number of participants will leave the course aware that they need more support than the course could provide. Have ready a short list of local grief support groups, hospice bereavement programs, mental health professionals who specialize in grief, and the 988 Suicide and Crisis Lifeline. Make this list available without singling anyone out.

A Note on the Group Continuing

Sometimes a group bonds deeply enough that participants want to keep meeting. This is fine if they want to organize it themselves. As the teacher, you do not need to lead an ongoing group, and the structure of this course is not designed for ongoing meeting. If participants want to keep gathering, they can do so on their own terms.

NOTES

REPRODUCIBLE HANDOUTS

Module 6

The following pages may be photocopied for classroom use.
Each handout is designed to fit a single 8.5 × 11 page.

HANDOUT 6A
Living Forward After a Loss
REPRODUCIBLE HANDOUT

A reference for the longer arc of grief, beyond the first weeks and months.

Anniversaries and Holidays

- First anniversary of the death is often the most intense.
- Birthdays, wedding anniversaries, and other meaningful dates can bring sharp returns.
- Holidays the deceased loved are especially difficult.
- The first time around the calendar is its own grieving process.

Secondary Losses

After the immediate loss, other losses surface that you did not anticipate: the loss of the future you imagined, the loss of identity, the loss of shared friends, the loss of a role you played in the family.

Rebuilding Daily Routines

Mealtimes, sleep, work, social rhythms — all need new shape. Rebuilding takes time. *Be patient.*

Honoring and Remembering

- Annual ritual visits to meaningful places
- A candle on the anniversary
- A favorite recipe prepared each year
- Charitable giving in the deceased's name
- A planted tree, a memorial bench, a piece of art
- Telling stories about the person, often, with people who knew them

Social Connections Rebuild Gradually

Some friendships will not survive. Other friends will surprise you. New friendships will form. The social world after major grief is different.

Life Direction Often Shifts

Many people who have been through significant grief find their priorities have changed. Trivial things shrink. Important things become more visible. **This is one of the gifts grief sometimes leaves.**

HANDOUT 6B

My Six-Month Plan

REPRODUCIBLE HANDOUT

Pick three specific commitments you will keep in the next six months. They should be concrete and realistic. Less is more.

Commitment 1

What I will do:

By when:

Who, if anyone, will know about this commitment (an accountability partner):

Commitment 2

What I will do:

By when:

Who, if anyone, will know about this commitment (an accountability partner):

Commitment 3

What I will do:

By when:

Who, if anyone, will know about this commitment (an accountability partner):

A REMINDER

Six months from now, look back at this list. Did you do what you said you would? If yes, choose three new commitments. If no, ask yourself why, and choose again. **The work continues.**

HANDOUT 6C

A Letter to My Future Self

REPRODUCIBLE HANDOUT

Write to yourself, to be opened in six months. There are no rules. Whatever you want your future self to know, write it. When you are done, fold this letter, seal it however you can, and write a date six months from today on the front. Take it home and put it somewhere you will find it.

DATE TODAY ______________________ **DATE TO OPEN** ______________________

Dear future me,

PART THREE

AFTER THE COURSE

Resources, references, and what comes next.

Course Resources

A list of resources to share with participants. Expand as needed for your local area.

Crisis and Mental Health Support

- **988 Suicide and Crisis Lifeline** (call or text 988)
- **Crisis Text Line** (text HOME to 741741)
- **SAMHSA National Helpline** (1-800-662-4357) for substance use or mental health

Grief Support

- Local hospice bereavement programs (most accept anyone in the community, not only families of hospice patients)
- **GriefShare** (griefshare.org) for in-person and online support groups
- **The Compassionate Friends** (compassionatefriends.org) for parents who have lost a child
- **Soaring Spirits International** (soaringspirits.org) for widowed people
- Local mental health professionals specializing in grief

Legal and Financial Help

- State and local bar associations for attorney referrals (most offer free or low-cost initial consultations)
- Legal aid organizations for those who cannot afford an attorney
- Certified financial planners through the CFP Board (cfp.net)
- AARP free legal and financial resources for older adults

End-of-Life Planning

- **Five Wishes** (fivewishes.org) for advance directive forms valid in most states
- **The Conversation Project** (theconversationproject.org) for guides on end-of-life talks
- **CaringInfo** (caringinfo.org) for state-specific advance directive forms

The Books and the App

- *When a Loved One Dies* · by Alice Truman
- *Not My Favorite Subject Either, But...* · by Alice Truman
- **LifeNowAndBeyond.com**

Teacher's Quick-Reference Card

A condensed reference for use during sessions. You may copy this page and keep it in front of you while teaching.

Ground Rules (Module 1)

1. What is shared here stays here.
2. You are never required to share.
3. We are not here to fix each other.
4. We use respectful language.

When to Refer

- **Self-harm or suicidal ideation:** 988 Lifeline. Speak privately after session.
- **Acute mental health crisis:** 988 or local emergency. Do not leave the person alone if immediate danger.
- **Legal questions:** Refer to attorney.
- **Financial questions:** Refer to certified financial planner or CPA.
- **Medical questions:** Refer to physician or hospice social worker.
- **Family conflict beyond the course:** Refer to mediator or family therapist.

Useful Phrases

- *"Take your time. We are with you."*
- *"Thank you for sharing that."*
- *"This is a lot. Let us take a breath together."*
- *"That is a great question for an attorney. The course points you to what to ask, not the answer."*
- *"What you are describing sounds heavy. Have you thought about talking to a grief counselor?"*

Six-Module Summary

- **Module 1** · The Conversation We Avoid — framing and group building
- **Module 2** · Getting Your Affairs in Order — the four pillars of preparation
- **Module 3** · The Immediate Aftermath — first 72 hours and service planning
- **Module 4** · Documents, Legal, and Digital Life — paperwork and digital legacy
- **Module 5** · Grief, Family, and Self-Care — emotional and relational journey
- **Module 6** · Moving Forward and Leaving a Legacy — living forward and closing

Timing

Recommended session length: 60 minutes. Reserve room for 90. Aim to end at 60. Allow occasional extension to 75 or 90 only when the moment calls for it. **Never go past 90.**

Index of Reproducible Handouts

All reproducible handouts in this guide, in order of use.

Module 6

Further Reading

and the Companion App

Suggestions for participants who want to continue the work after the course ends.

Return to the Books

Both *When a Loved One Dies* and *Not My Favorite Subject Either, But...* reward repeated reading. Specific chapters that participants often find more useful the second time around include:

- **From** *When a Loved One Dies***:** Chapter 7 (Grief and the Family Circle), Chapter 12 (Life After the Funeral), and Chapter 13 (Preparing for the Future)
- **From** *Not My Favorite Subject Either, But...***:** Chapter 12 (Living Well Until the End), Chapter 13 (The Before I Die Master Checklist), and Chapter 14 (Your Personalized Plan)

Continued Use of the App

The Life Now and Beyond app is designed for ongoing use. Encourage participants to:

- Update their Life Binder at least annually — personal information, medical updates, beneficiary changes, account changes
- Maintain their Trusted Access contacts and permissions as their family situation changes
- Continue using the Before Journey at their own pace, returning to chapters that fit their current focus
- Use Conversation Starters to support continued family discussions
- Track progress on six-month commitments in the Planning Journal
- Create Remembrance Pages (premium) to honor loved ones who have passed
- Return to the app whenever life changes — a new child, a new home, a new job, a death in the family, a serious illness
- Consider upgrading to premium ($49/year) if the four premium Life Binder sections (Insurance, Financial, Legal, Digital Legacy) and the After-Loss Guidance & Support workspace would meaningfully complete their preparation

A Word to the Teacher

You have just walked a small group of people through some of the most important work they will ever do.

Take a moment, after the final session, to acknowledge what you have done. This work matters. The participants you taught now have a structure for facing what most people refuse to face. They will pass that on to their families and their friends.

Whether you teach this course once or many times, you are making a real contribution to the people in your community. Thank you for taking it on.

Thank you for teaching.

This work matters.

Made in United States
Orlando, FL
05 November 2026

90209467R00070